GENESIS

Chapters 1—15

J. Vernon McGee

THOMAS NELSON PUBLISHERS

Nashville • Atlanta • London • Vancouver

Published in Nashville, Tennessee, by Thomas Nelson, Inc.

Scripture quotations are from the KING JAMES VERSION of the Bible.

Library of Congress Cataloging-in-Publication Data

McGee, J. Vernon (John Vernon), 1904–1988
    [Thru the Bible with J. Vernon McGee]
    Thru the Bible commentary series / J. Vernon McGee.
      p.   cm.
    Reprint. Originally published: Thru the Bible with J. Vernon
McGee. 1975.
    Includes bibliographical references.
    ISBN 0-7852-1001-6 (TR)
    ISBN 0-7852-1067-9 (NRM)
    1. Bible—Commentaries. I. Title.
BS491.2.M37 1991
220.7'7—dc20   90–41340
                                             CIP

PRINTED IN MEXICO
20 21 22 23 - 06

CONTENTS

GENESIS—CHAPTERS 1—15

PREFACE

The radio broadcasts of the Thru the Bible Radio five-year program were transcribed, edited, and published first in single-volume paperbacks to accommodate the radio audience.

There has been a minimal amount of further editing for this publication. Therefore, these messages are not the word-for-word recording of the taped messages which went out over the air. The changes were necessary to accommodate a reading audience rather than a listening audience.

These are popular messages, prepared originally for a radio audience. They should not be considered a commentary on the entire Bible in any sense of that term. These messages are devoid of any attempt to present a theological or technical commentary on the Bible. Behind these messages is a great deal of research and study in order to interpret the Bible from a popular rather than from a scholarly (and too-often boring) viewpoint.

We have definitely and deliberately attempted "to put the cookies on the bottom shelf so that the kiddies could get them."

The fact that these messages have been translated into many languages for radio broadcasting and have been received with enthusiasm reveals the need for a simple teaching of the whole Bible for the masses of the world.

I am indebted to many people and to many sources for bringing this volume into existence. I should express my especial thanks to my secretary, Gertrude Cutler, who supervised the editorial work; to Dr. Elliott R. Cole, my associate, who handled all the detailed work with the publishers; and finally, to my wife Ruth for tenaciously encouraging me from the beginning to put my notes and messages into printed form.

Solomon wrote, ". . . of making many books there is no end; and much study is a weariness of the flesh" (Eccl. 12:12). On a sea of books that flood the marketplace, we launch this series of THRU THE BIBLE with the hope that it might draw many to the one Book, *The Bible*.

J. Vernon McGee

GUIDELINES FOR BIBLE STUDY

INTRODUCTION

Is the Bible Important?

The Bible is probably the most maligned Book that ever has been written. It has been attacked as no other book has ever been attacked. Yet it has ministered and does minister to literally millions of people around the globe, and it has been doing this now for several thousand years. A Book of this nature and with this tremendous impact upon the human family certainly deserves the intelligent consideration of men and women.

Sir Walter Scott, on his deathbed, asked Lockhart to read to him. Puzzled, as he scanned the shelf of books that Walter Scott had written, he asked, "What book shall I read?" And Sir Walter replied, "Why do you ask that question? There is but one book; bring the Bible." There is only one Book for any man who is dying, but it is also *the* Book for any man who is living. A great many folk do not get interested in the Bible until they get to the end of their lives or until they get into a great deal of difficulty. While it is wonderful to have a Book in which you can find comfort in a time like that, it is also a Book for you to *live*—in the full vigor of life. It is a Book to face life with today, and it's the Book which furnishes the only sure route through this world and on into the next world. It is the only Book that can enable us to meet the emergencies and cushion the shocks that come to us in life. The Bible is different from any other book.

That this Book has influenced great men who in turn have influenced the world is evident. Let me share with you some quotations.

There was an African prince who came to England and was presented to Her Majesty Queen Victoria. This prince asked a very significant question, "What is the secret of England's greatness?" The queen got a beautifully bound copy of the Bible and presented it to the prince with this statement. "This is the secret of England's greatness." I wonder if England's decline to a second-rate and then third-rate nation may be tied up in the fact that England has gotten away from the Word of God.

Prime Minister Gladstone, probably one of the greatest legal minds Britain ever produced, said, "Talk about the questions of the day! There is but one question, and that is the Gospel. That can and will correct everything. I am glad to say that about all the men at the top in Great Britain are Christians . . . I have been in public position fifty-eight years, all but eleven of them in the cabinet of the British government, and during those forty-seven years have been associated with sixty of the master minds of the century, and all but five of the sixty were Christians." I personally think that part of the problems we are having in the world today is that we have too few Christians at the top, too few who are acquainted with the Word of God.

Michael Faraday, perhaps the greatest scientist of the early 1800s, said, "But why will people go astray, when they have this blessed book of God to guide them?" Sir Isaac Newton, a scientist in the preceding century, said, "If the Bible is true, the time is coming when men shall travel at fifty miles an hour." And Voltaire, the French skeptic, commented, "Poor Isaac. He was in his dotage when he made that prophecy. It only shows what Bible study will do to an otherwise scientific mind."

It might be interesting to note what some of our early presidents had to say about the Bible. John Adams, our second president, said, "I have examined all [that is, all of Scripture] as well as my narrow sphere, my straightened means, and my busy life will allow me, and the result is that the Bible is the best book in the world. It contains more of my little philosophy than all the libraries I have seen, and such parts of it I cannot reconcile to my little philosophy I postpone for further investigation." President John Quincy Adams said, "I speak as a man of the world to men of the world; and I say to you: Search the Scriptures. The Bible is the book above all others to be read at all ages and in all conditions of human life; not to be read once or twice through then laid aside, but to be read in small portions every day." And the presidents back in those days, who made our nation great, did not get us into foreign wars and were able to solve the problems of the streets. Someone may counter, "But the problems weren't as complicated then as they are now." They were for that day, friend. Not only England but also the United States has gotten away from the Word of God. And the farther we get, the more complicated our problems become. Right now there are men in positions of authority in this land who are saying that there is no solution to our problems. That is the reason I am teaching the Word of God in its entirety—I believe it is the only solution. And, frankly, friend, we had better get back to it.

Another president, Thomas Jefferson, said, "I have always said, and always will say, that the studious perusal of the Sacred Volume will make better citizens, better husbands, and better fathers." This is something to think over today when our citizens are burning down the cities in which they live and when divorce is running rife.

Daniel Webster made this statement: "If there be anything in my style or thoughts to be commended, the credit is due to my kind parents for instilling into my mind an early love of the Scriptures." What about you today, Christian parent? Are you making a Daniel Webster in your home or a little rebel? Webster also made this statement: "I have read it [the Bible] through many times. I now make a practice of going through it once a year. It is the Book of all others for lawyers as well as divines. I pity the man who cannot find in it a rich supply of thought and rules for conduct."

Born in the East and clothed in Oriental form and imagery, the Bible walks the ways of all the world with familiar feet, and enters land after land to find its own everywhere. It has learned to speak in hundreds of languages to the heart of man. It comes into the palace to tell the monarch that he is a servant of the Most High, and into the cottage to assure the peasant that he is a son of God. Children listen to its stories with wonder and delight, and wise men ponder them as parables of life. It has a word of peace for the time of peril, a word of comfort for the time of calamity, a word of light for the hour of darkness. Its oracles are repeated in the assembly of the people, and its counsels whispered in the ear of the lonely. The wicked and the proud tremble at its warnings, but to the wounded and the penitent it has a mother's voice. The wilderness and the solitary place have been made glad by it, and the fire on the hearth has lit the reading of its well-worn pages. It has woven itself into our dearest dreams; so that love, friendship, sympathy and devotion, memory and hope put on the beautiful garments of its treasured speech, breathing of frankincense and myrrh.

—Henry van Dyke

In What Way Is the Bible Unique?

In many ways the Bible is a most unusual Book. For instance, it has a dual authorship. In other words, God is the Author of the Bible, and in another sense man is the author of the Bible. Actually, the Bible was written by about forty authors over a period of approximately fifteen hundred years. Some of these men never even heard of the others, and there was no collusion among the forty. Two or three of them could have gotten together, but the others could not have known each other. And yet they have presented a Book that has the most marvelous continuity of any book that has ever been written. Also, it is without error. Each author expressed his own feelings in his own generation. Each has his limitations, and made his mistakes—poor old Moses made mistakes, but when he was writing the Pentateuch, somehow or other no mistakes got in there. You see, it is a human Book and yet it is a God-Book.

It is a very human Book, written by men from all walks of life, prince and pauper, the highly intellectual and the very simple. For example, Dr. Luke writes almost classical Greek in a period when the Koine Greek was popular. His Greek is marvelous! But Simon Peter, the fisherman, wrote some Greek also. He is not so good, but God the Holy Spirit used both of these men. He let them express exactly their thoughts, their feelings, and yet through that method the Spirit of God was able to overrule in such a way that God said exactly what He wanted to say. That's the wonder of the Book, the Bible.

It is a God-Book. In the Bible God says twenty-five hundred times, "God said . . . the Lord has said . . . thus saith the Lord," and so on. God has made it very clear that He is speaking through this Book. It is a Book that can communicate life to you. You can even become a child of God, begotten "not by corruptible seed, but by incorruptible, by the Word of God that liveth and abideth forever." It is God's communication to man. And if God spoke out of heaven right now, He would just repeat Himself because He has said all that He wants to say to this generation. And, by the way, He didn't learn anything when He read the morning paper. When man went to the moon, he didn't discover anything that God didn't already know when He gave us the Bible. He is the same God who created this universe that we are in today.

The Bible is both divine and human. In a way it is like my Lord who walked down here and grew weary and sat down at a well. Although He was God, He was man. He talked with people down here and communicated with them. This is a Book that communicates. It speaks to mankind today. The Bible is for men as they are.

The Bible is a corridor between two eternities down which walks the Christ of God; his invisible steps echo through the Old Testament, but we meet Him face to face in the throne room of the New; and it is through that Christ alone, crucified for me, that I have found forgiveness for sins and life eternal. The Old Testament is summed up in the word Christ; the New Testament is summed up in the word Jesus; and the summary of the whole Bible is that Jesus is the Christ.

—Bishop Pollock

How Do You Know the Bible Is From God?

This is a good question, and it should be asked and answered.

1. Preservation—One of the objective proofs, one of the external proofs, has been the marvelous preservation of the Bible. There was a king of old—we read about him in Jeremiah—who, when the Word was sent to him, took a penknife and cut it to pieces. But it was rewritten, and we have that Word today. Down through the centuries there have been a great many Bible burnings. Today there's a great deal of antagonism toward the Bible. In our country today it is not being burned because we think that we are too civilized for such behavior. The way enemies of God's Word try to get rid of it is just to outlaw it in our schools and in many other places. (Yet we talk about our freedom of religion and freedom of speech.) In spite of all the attacks that have been made upon the Bible, it still today exists—and, of course, it's one of the best-sellers. For many years it was *the* best-seller, but it's not today. I regret to have to say that, but it is true. And that is certainly a commentary on our contemporary society. It reveals that the Bible is not really occupying the place that it once did in the history and in the life of of this nation. Yet, I think the amazing preservation of the Word of God is worthy of consideration.

2. Archaeology—Another way in which we know the Bible is the Word of God is through archaeology. The spade of the archaeologist has turned up many things that have proven that this Book is the Word of God. For instance, critics for many years denied the Mosaic authorship of the Pentateuch on the basis that writing was not in existence in Moses' day. You haven't heard anybody advance that theory recently, have you? Well, of course not. For years the spade of the archaeologist has turned up again and again evidence of the validity of the Bible. The city of Jericho and the walls that fell down are one example. Now there has been some argument between Miss Kathleen Kenyon and Sir Charles Marsdon relative to specifics, but it's well established that the walls fell down, and I'll let them debate about the time and all that sort of thing. The Word of God has been substantiated there, and in many other ways archaeology has demonstrated the accuracy of the Bible. Many of the manuscripts that have been found do that also. It's quite interesting that when the Isaiah Scrolls, the Dead Sea Scrolls, were found, the liberal leaped at that because he thought he had found an argument that would discredit the Bible. However, the scrolls have not discredited the Bible, and it seems that the liberal has lost a great deal of interest in them. This is a field into which you might do some research, as I cannot go to any great length in this brief study.

3. Fulfilled Prophecy—If I were asked today whether I had just one thing to suggest as a conclusive proof that the Bible is the Word of God, do you know what I would suggest? I would suggest fulfilled prophecy. Fulfilled prophecy is the one proof that you can't escape, you can't get around. And the Bible is full of fulfilled prophecy. One-fourth of Scripture, when it was written, was prophetic; that is, it an-nounced things that were to take place in the future. A great deal of that—in fact, a great deal more than people imagine—has already been fulfilled. We could turn to many places where prophecy has been fulfilled exactly. We find that there were many local situations that were fulfilled even in the day of the prophet. For example, Micaiah was the prophet who told Ahab that if he went out to battle as he planned, he would lose the battle and would be killed. However, Ahab's false prophets had told him he'd have a victory and would return as a victorious king. Because he didn't like what Micaiah said, Ahab ordered him locked up and fed bread and water, and said he would take care of him when he got back. But Micaiah shot back the last word, "If you come back at all, the Lord hasn't spoken by me." Well, evidently the Lord had spoken by him because Ahab didn't come back. He was killed in the battle, and his army was defeated. He had even disguised himself so that there would be no danger of his losing his life. But an enemy soldier, the Scripture says, pulled his bow at a venture; that is, when the battle was about over, he had just one arrow left in his quiver; he put it in place and shot, not really aiming at anything. But, you know, that arrow must have had Ahab's name on it, and it found him. It went right to its mark. Why? Because Micaiah had made an accurate prophecy (1 Kings 22).

On another occasion, the prophet Isaiah said that the invading Assyrian army wouldn't shoot an arrow into the city of Jerusalem (2 Kings 19:32). Well now, that's interesting. Micaiah's prophecy was fulfilled because a soldier shot an arrow by chance, pulled his bow at a venture. Wouldn't you think that among two hundred thousand soldiers—that "great host"—perhaps one might be trigger-happy and would pull his bow at a venture and let an arrow fly over the wall of Jerusalem? Well, he didn't. If the enemy had shot an arrow inside that city, they could be sure that Isaiah was not God's prophet. But he was, as was proven by this local fulfillment of his prophecy. But Isaiah also said a virgin would bring forth a child, and that was seven hundred years before it was literally fulfilled. And then, if you want a final proof, there were over three hundred prophecies concerning the first coming of Christ which were all literally fulfilled. As Jesus Christ was hanging there on the Cross and dying, there was one prophecy recorded in the Old Testament that had not been fulfilled. It was, "They gave me vinegar to drink" (Ps. 69:21). Jesus said, "I thirst," and the enemy himself went and fulfilled prophecy (John 19:28–30). It's a most amazing thing. Men can't guess like that.

It has been rather amusing to watch the weatherman. During the summer season in Southern California he does fine, but when we get to the change of seasons—well, your guess is as good as his. In the nation Israel, a prophet had to be accurate. If he was not accurate, he was to be put to death as a false prophet. God told His people that they would be able to distinguish a false prophet from a true prophet. A true prophet must first speak to a local situation, which Isaiah did. When that prophecy came to pass, they would know they could trust him to speak concerning the future, as Isaiah did. We can look back now and know that it was fulfilled.

There are so many other prophecies. Tyre and Sidon are over there today exactly as God's Word said twenty-five hundred years ago they would be. Egypt today is in the exact position God said it would be in. All of these are amazing, friend, and fulfilled prophecy is one of the greatest proofs that the Bible is indeed the Word of God. You see, men just can't be that accurate. Men can't guess like that—even the weatherman misses it.

Let me show you that, according to mathematical law of problematical conjecture, man could never, never prophesy. Suppose that right now I would make a prophecy. Just by way of illustration, suppose I'd say that wherever you are it's going to rain tomorrow. I'd have a 50 percent chance of being right because it'll do one of the two. But suppose that I add to that and say it would start raining tomorrow morning at nine o'clock. That would be another uncertain element. I had a fifty-fifty chance of being right at first; now I have perhaps a 25 percent chance. Every uncertain element that is added reduces by at least 50 percent the chance of my being right—the law of problematical conjecture. Now suppose that I not only say that it's going to start raining at nine o'clock, but I also say it'll stop raining at two o'clock. That has reduced my chances now another 50 percent, which brings it down to 12½ percent. Can you imagine my chance of being right now? But suppose I add three hundred uncertain elements. There's not a ghost of a chance of my being accurate. I just couldn't hit it—it would be impossible. Yet the Word of God hit it, my friend. It is accurate. The Bible has moved into that area of absolute impossibility, and that to me is absolute proof that it is the Word of God. There is nothing to compare to it at all. I have given very few examples of fulfilled prophecy, but there is in the Word of God prophecy after prophecy, and they have been fulfilled—literally fulfilled. And by the way, I would think that that indicates the method in which prophecy for the future is yet to be fulfilled.

4. Transformed Lives—I offer two final reasons as proof that the Bible is the Word of God. One is the transformed lives of believers today. I have seen what the Word of God can do in the lives of men and women. I'm thinking right now of a man in Oakland, California, who listened to my Bible-teaching program. He probably had as many problems, as many hang-ups, and he was in as much sin as any man that I know anything about. And this man began to listen to the radio program. I know of people who just hear the gospel once and are converted. I think it's possible and that it's wonderful. But this man listened to it week after week, and he became antagonistic. He became angry. Later he said to me, "If I could have gotten to you when you were teaching the Epistle to the Romans and you told me that I was a sinner, I would have hit you in the nose," and frankly, I think he could have done it. He's much bigger and much younger than I am. I'm glad he couldn't get to me. Finally, this man turned to Christ. It has been wonderful to see what God has done in his life. Again and again and again this testimony could be multiplied. Young and old have found purpose and fulfillment in life, marriages have been saved, families reunited, individuals have been freed from alcoholism and drug addiction. Folk have had their lives transformed by coming to Christ.

When I finished seminary, I was a preacher who majored in the realm of the defense of the gospel, and I attempted to defend the Bible. In fact, I think every message I gave entered into that area. I felt if I could just get enough answers to the questions that people raise for not believing the Bible, they would believe. But I found out that the worst thing I could do was to whip a man down intellectually. The minute I did that, I made an enemy and never could win him for the Lord. So I moved out of the realm of apologetics and into another area of just giving out the Word of God as simply as I could. Only the Bible can turn a sinner into a saint.

5. Spirit of God Made It Real—Another reason that I've moved out of the realm of apologetics is because there has been a certain development in my own life. I have reached the place today where I not only believe that the Bible is the Word of God, I *know* it's the Word of God. I know it's the Word of God because the Spirit of God has made it real to my own heart and my own life. That is the thing that Paul talked to the Colossians about. He prayed that they "might be filled with the knowledge of his will in all wisdom and spiritual understanding." I also want this, because I found that the Spirit of God can confirm these things to your heart and you don't need archaeology or anything else to prove that the Bible is God's Word.

A young preacher said to me some time ago, "Dr. McGee, isn't it wonderful that they have discovered this?" He mentioned a recent discovery in particular.

And I said, "Well, I don't see anything to be excited about."

He was greatly disappointed and even chagrined that I did not respond enthusiastically. "Why, what do you mean?" he asked. "Is it possible that this hasn't impressed you?"

I answered him this way, "I already knew it was the Word of God long before the spade of the archaeologist turned that up." He asked how I knew it, and I said, "The Spirit of God has been making it real to my own heart."

I trust that the Spirit of God is going to make the Word of God not only real to you, to incorporate it into your living, but that He is also going to give you that assurance that you can say, "I *know* that it's the Word of God."

> Whence but from Heaven, could men unskilled in arts,
> In several ages born, in several parts,
> Weave such agreeing truths, or how, or why,
> Should all conspire to cheat us with a lie?

Unasked their pains, ungrateful their advice,
Starving their gain, and martyrdom their price.

—Dryden

What Is Revelation? Inspiration? Illumination? Interpretation?

Revelation means that God has spoken and that God has communicated to man. *Inspiration* guarantees the revelation of God. *Illumination* has to do with the Spirit of God being the Teacher—He communicates. *Interpretation* has to do with the interpretation that you and I give to the Word of God.

Revelation

Revelation means that God has spoken. "Thus saith the Lord," and its equivalent, occurs over twenty-five hundred times. The Lord didn't want you to misunderstand that He had spoken. Notice Hebrews 1:1–2: "God, who at sundry times and in divers manners spake in time past unto the fathers by the prophets, hath in these last days spoken unto us by his Son, whom he hath appointed heir of all things, by whom also he made the worlds." Wherever you will find two persons, endowed with a reasonable degree of intelligence, who harbor the same feelings and desires, who are attracted to each other more or less, you will find communication between them. Persons of like propensities, separated from each other, delight in getting in touch with each other and rejoice in receiving communication from each other. This innate characteristic of the human heart explains the post office department, the telephone, and the telegraph. Friends communicate with friends. A husband away from home writes to his wife. A boy or girl at school will write home to dad and mom. And ever and anon there travels the scented epistle of a girl to a boy, and then the boy returns an epistle to the girl. All of this is called communication. It is the expression of the heart. I remember the thrill that came to me when I read the account of Helen Keller, shut out from the world by blindness and deafness, without means of communication; and then a way was opened up so she could communicate—probably better than many of us who can see and hear.

Now, on the basis of all this, I would like to ask you what I believe is a reasonable and certainly an intelligent question: Isn't it reasonable to conclude that God has communicated with His creatures to whom He has committed a certain degree of intelligence and whom He created in His likeness? If we did not have a revelation from God, right now I think that you and I could just wait and He would be speaking to us, because we could *expect* God to speak to us. You will notice that the writer to the Hebrews says that God in the Old Testament spoke through the prophets, and He now has spoken through Christ. Both the revelation to the prophets in the Old Testament and the revelation of Christ in the New Testament are in the Word of God, of course, and that is the only way we would know about the communication from either one. The Bible has sixty-six books, and God has spoken to us through each one of them.

This Book contains the mind of God, the state of man, the way of salvation, the doom of sinners and the happiness of believers. Its doctrines are holy, its precepts are binding, its histories are true, and its decisions are immutable. Read it to be wise, believe it to be safe and practice it to be holy. It contains light to direct you, food to support you and comfort to cheer you. It is the traveler's map, the pilgrim's staff, the pilot's compass, the soldier's sword and the Christian's character. Here paradise is restored, heaven opened and the gates of hell disclosed. Christ is its grand object, our good is its design and the glory of God its end. It should fill the memory, rule the heart, and guide the feet. Read it slowly, frequently, and prayerfully. It is given you in life and will be opened in the judgment and will be remembered forever. It involves the highest responsibility, will reward the greatest labour, and will condemn all who trifle with its sacred contents.

—Author Unknown

Inspiration

This brings us to the second great subject, which is *inspiration*. I personally believe in what is known as the plenary verbal inspiration of the Scriptures, which means that the Bible is an authoritative statement and that every word of it is the Word of God to us and for us in this day in which we live. Inspiration guarantees the revelation of God. And that is exactly what this Book says. Two men—Paul writing his last epistle to Timothy and Peter writing his last epistle—had something pretty definite to say about the Bible: "All scripture is given by inspiration of God, and is profitable for doctrine, for reproof, for correction, for instruction in righteousness: That the man of God may be perfect, thoroughly furnished unto all good works" (2 Tim. 3:16–17, New Scofield Reference Bible). Notice that *all* Scripture is given by inspiration. The word *inspiration* means "God breathed." God said through these men, as He said here through Paul, exactly what He wanted to say. He hasn't anything else to add. Peter expresses it this way: "For the prophecy came not in old time by the will of man: but holy men of God spake as they were moved by the Holy Ghost" (2 Pet. 1:21). It is very important to see that these men were moved, as it were, carried along, by the Holy Spirit of God. It was Bishop Westcott who said, "The thoughts are wedded to words as necessarily as the soul is to the body." And Dr. Keiper said, "You can as easily have music without notes, or mathematics without figures, as thoughts without words." It is not the thoughts that are inspired; it's the *words* that are inspired.

There is a little whimsical story of a girl who had taken singing lessons from a very famous teacher. He was present at her recital, and after it was over she was anxious to know his reaction. He didn't come to congratulate her, and she asked a friend, "What did he say?"

Her loyal friend answered, "He said that you sang heavenly."

She couldn't quite believe that her teacher had said that; so she probed, "Is that *exactly* what he said?"

"Well, no, but that is what he meant."

The girl insisted, "Tell me the exact *words* that he used."

"Well, his exact words were, 'That was an unearthly noise!'"

Obviously, there is a difference between an unearthly noise and a heavenly sound. Exact words are important.

Believe me, the words of Scripture are inspired—not just the thoughts, but the words. For instance, Satan was not inspired to tell a lie, but the Bible records that he told a lie. It's the words that are inspired. And the Lord Jesus often said, "It is written," quoting the Word of God in the Old Testament—the men who wrote gave out what God had to say. In Exodus 20:1 Moses wrote: "And God spake all these words, saying . . . ." It was God who did the speaking, and Moses wrote what He said.

Over the years there have been discovered many very excellent manuscripts of the Scriptures. Speaking of the manuscripts in Britain, Sir George Kenyon, the late director and principal librarian of the British Museum, made this statement: "Thanks to these manuscripts, the ordinary reader of the Bible may feel comfortable about the soundness of the text. Apart from a few unimportant verbal alterations, natural in books transcribed by hand, the New Testament, we now feel assured, has come down intact." We can be sure today that we have that which is as close to the autographs (the original manuscripts) as anything possibly can be, and I believe in verbal plenary inspiration of the autographs.

In the second century Irenaeus, one of the church fathers, wrote: "The Scriptures indeed are perfect, forasmuch as they are spoken by the Word of God and by His Spirit." Augustine, living in the fifth century, made this statement, "Let us therefore yield ourselves and bow to the authority of the Holy Scriptures which can neither err nor deceive." And Spurgeon commented, "I can never doubt the doctrine of plenary verbal inspiration; since I so constantly see, in actual practice, how the very words that God has been pleased to use—a plural instead of a singular—are blessed to the souls of men." God speaks in this Book to our hearts and to our lives.

Illumination

Illumination means that since you and I have a Book, a God-Book and a human Book, written by men who were expressing their thoughts and at the same time writing down the Word of God, only the Spirit of God can teach it to us. Although we can get the facts of the Bible on our own, the Spirit of God will have to open our minds and hearts if we are to understand the spiritual truth that is there.

Paul, writing to the Corinthians, said, "But we speak the wisdom of God in a mystery, even the hidden wisdom, which God ordained before the world unto our glory: Which none of the princes of this world knew: for had they known it, they would not have crucified the Lord of glory. But as it is written, Eye hath not seen, nor ear heard, neither have entered into the heart of man, the things which God hath prepared for them that love him" (1 Cor. 2:7–9). Now you and I get most of what we know through the eye gate and the ear gate or by reason. Paul tells us here that there are certain things that eye has not seen nor ear heard, certain things that you can't get into your mind at all. Then how in the world are you going to get them? "But God hath revealed them unto us by his Spirit: for the Spirit searcheth all things, yea, the deep things of God" (1 Cor. 2:10). Verse 9 sometimes goes to a funeral. The minister implies that the one who has died didn't know too much down here, but now he will know things he did not know before. While that probably is true (we will get quite an education in heaven), that is not what the verse literally says. Long before you get to the undertaker, there are a lot of things in this life that you and I can't learn through natural means. The Holy Spirit has to be our Teacher.

Remember that our Lord inquired of His disciples, "What are men saying about Me?" They said that some were saying one thing and some another. (And today you can get a different answer from almost every person you happen to ask. There are many viewpoints of Him.) Then He asked His disciples, ". . . But whom say ye that I am? And Simon Peter answered and said, Thou art the Christ, the Son of the living God. And Jesus answered and said unto him, Blessed art thou, Simon Bar-jona: for flesh and blood hath not revealed it unto thee, but my Father which is in heaven" (Matt. 16:15–17). God is the One who revealed the truth to Simon Peter. And today only God can open up the Word of God for us to really understand it.

On the day of the resurrection of the Lord Jesus, He walked down the Emmaus road and joined a couple of men as they walked along. Entering into their conversation, He asked them, ". . . What manner of communications are these that ye had one to another, as ye walk, and are sad? And the one of them, whose name was Cleopas, answering said unto him, Art thou only a stranger in Jerusalem, and hast not known the things which are come to pass there in these days? And he said unto them, What things? And they said unto him, Concerning

Jesus of Nazareth, which was a prophet mighty in deed and word before God and all the people: And how the chief priests and our rulers delivered him to be condemned to death, and have crucified him" (Luke 24:17–20). As you will recall, Jesus had predicted that. And it is interesting to see that written prophecy had been saying it for years. Then they expressed the hope that had been theirs: "But we trusted that it had been he which should have redeemed Israel: and beside all this, today is the third day since these things were done" (Luke 24:21). And they went on to tell about what they knew and what the women had reported: those who "were with us went to the sepulchre . . . but him they saw not" (Luke 24:24). Their hopes had dimmed, and darkness had entered their hearts. Now listen to the Lord Jesus, ". . . O fools, and slow of heart to believe all that the prophets have spoken: Ought not Christ to have suffered these things, and to enter into his glory? And beginning at Moses and all the prophets, he expounded unto them in all the scriptures the things concerning himself" (Luke 24:25–27). Wouldn't you have loved to have been there that day and heard Him go back in the Old Testament and lift out the Scriptures concerning Himself? And after He finally made Himself known to them as they sat at the evening meal, this was their comment, ". . . Did not our heart burn within us, while he talked with us by the way, and while he opened to us the scriptures?" (Luke 24:32).

You see, we are studying a Book that is different from any other book. I not only believe in the inspiration of the Bible, I believe that it is a closed Book to you unless the Spirit of God will open your heart and make it real. When Jesus returned to Jerusalem at that time, He continued teaching the disciples: "And he said unto them, These are the words which I spake unto you, while I was yet with you, that all things must be fulfilled, which were written in the law of Moses, and in the prophets, and in the psalms, concerning me" (Luke 24:44). Notice that He believed Moses wrote the Pentateuch; He believed the prophets spoke of Him and that the Psalms pointed to Him. Now here is the important verse: "Then opened he their understanding, that they might understand the scriptures" (Luke 24:45). And, friend, if He doesn't open your understanding, you're just not going to get it.

That is the reason we ought to approach this Book with great humility of mind, regardless of how high our I.Q. is or the extent of our education.

Referring back to 1 Corinthians, Paul goes on to say, "Which things also we speak, not in the words which man's wisdom teacheth, but which the Holy Spirit teacheth; comparing spiritual things with spiritual. But the natural man receiveth not the things of the Spirit of God: for they are foolishness unto him: neither can he know them, because they are spiritually discerned" (1 Cor. 2:13–14, New Scofield Reference Bible). I am never disturbed when one of these unbelievers, even if he's a preacher, comes along and says he no longer believes the Bible is the Word of God; that's the way he *should* talk. After all, if he is not a believer, he cannot understand it. Mark Twain, who was no believer, said that he was not disturbed by what he did not understand in the Bible; what worried him were the things he *did* understand. There are things an unbeliever can understand, and it's those things which cause many to reject the Word of God. It was Pascal who said, "Human knowledge must be understood to be loved, but Divine knowledge must be loved to be understood."

As I leave the subject of illumination, let me add this: Only the Spirit of God can open your mind and heart to see and to accept Christ and to trust Him as your Savior. How wonderful! I have always felt as I entered the pulpit how helpless I am; believe me, Vernon McGee can't convert anyone. But I not only feel weak, I also feel mighty—not mighty in myself, but in the knowledge that the Spirit of God can take my dead words and make them real and living.

Interpretation

Interpretation has to do with the interpretation that you and I give to the Word of God. And this is the reason there are Methodists and Baptists and Presbyterians, this kind of teacher and that kind of teacher—we all have our interpretations. And where there is disagreement, somebody is evidently wrong.

There are several rules that should be followed as we attempt to interpret the Bible.

1. The overall purpose of the Bible should first be considered.

And that is the reason I teach all of it—because I believe you need to have it all before you can come to any dogmatic conclusion concerning any particular verse of Scripture. It is important to take into consideration all verses that are related to that subject.

2. To whom the Scripture is addressed should next be considered. For instance, way back yonder God said to Joshua, "Arise, go over this Jordan" (Josh. 1:2). When I was over in that land, I crossed the Jordan River, but I didn't cross it to fulfill that Scripture. And I didn't say, "At last I've obeyed the Lord and have crossed over Jordan." No. When I read that verse I know the Lord is talking to Joshua—but I believe there is a tremendous lesson there for me. All Scripture is not *to* me, but all Scripture is *for* me. That is a good rule to keep in mind.

3. The immediate context before and after a Scripture should be observed. What is the passage talking about? And what other passages of Scripture deal with the same thing?

4. Discover what the original says. If you do not read Hebrew or Greek, when you read the American Standard Version you're right close to what the Lord said. Frankly, I cannot recommend the modern translations, although there are good things in them. I have found that because we are so divided doctrinally, every group that attempts to translate the Bible just naturally injects into their translation their particular viewpoint. Therefore, if the liberal is going to do the translating, you may get a taste of liberalism. If the fundamentalist is going to do the translating, you'll get his bias in certain places. However, the men who did the original English translations were men who believed that the Bible was the Word of God and handled it accordingly. When there were words they could not translate, they simply transliterated them (for instance, *Abba* and *baptizo*). The danger in modern translations is that translation is done in a dogmatic fashion. A translator must take something out of one language and put it into another language in comparable terms—identical terms if possible. Most of our modern translators are trying to get it into modern speech. And in doing so, they really miss what the original is saying. Personally, I stick by the Authorized (King James) Version. I feel that The New Scofield Reference Bible has made a tremendous step forward in making certain distinctions and corrections that needed to be made in the Au-

thorized Version. I recommend that also, although I still use my old
Scofield Reference Bible. I know my way around through the Book,
and the old scout will follow the old trail. However, the important
thing is to attempt to determine the exact words of the original.

5. Interpret the Bible literally. The late Dr. David Cooper has
stated it well: "When the plain sense of Scripture makes common
sense, seek no other sense; therefore, take every word at its primary,
ordinary, usual, literal meaning unless the facts of the immediate context, studied in the light of related passages and axiomatic and fundamental truths, indicate clearly otherwise."

Guidelines

**"Open thou mine eyes, that I may behold wondrous
things out of thy law" [Ps. 119:18].**

There are certain guidelines that each of us should follow relative to
the Word of God. I guarantee that if you will follow these guidelines,
blessing will come to your heart and life. Certainly there should be
these directions in the study of Scripture. Today a bottle of medicine,
no matter how simple it might be, has directions for the use of it. And
any little gadget that you buy in a five-and-ten-cent store has with it
directions for its operation. If that is true of the things of this world,
certainly the all-important Word of God should have a few directions
and instructions on the study of it. I want to mention seven very simple, yet basic, preliminary steps that will be a guide for the study of
the Word of God.

1. Begin with prayer.
2. Read the Bible.
3. Study the Bible.
4. Meditate on the Bible.
5. Read what others have written on the Bible.
6. Obey the Bible.
7. Pass it on to others.

You may want to add to these, but I believe these are basic and
primary. Someone has put it in a very brief, cogent manner: "The

Bible—know it in your head; stow it in your heart; show it in your life; sow it in the world." That is another way of saying some of the things we are going to present here.

1. Begin with Prayer.

As we saw when we dealt with the subject of illumination, the Bible differs from other books in that the Holy Spirit alone can open our minds to understand it. You can take up a book on philosophy, and if a man wrote it (and he did), then a man can understand it. The same is true of higher mathematics or any other subject. There is not a book that ever has been written by any man that another man cannot understand. But the Bible is different. The Bible cannot be understood unless the Holy Spirit is the instructor. And He *wants* to teach us. The fact of the matter is, our Lord told us, ". . . He will guide you into all truth" (John 16:13). When we open the Word of God we need to begin with the psalmist's prayer: "Open thou mine eyes, that I may behold wondrous things out of thy law" (Ps. 119:18). When the psalmist wrote these lines, he had in mind the Mosaic system, of course; but we widen that out to include the sixty-six books of the Bible and pray today, "Open thou mine eyes, that I may behold wondrous things out of thy Word."

When the apostle Paul was praying for the Ephesians, he did not pray for their health (although he may have at another time), and he did not pray that they might get wealthy (I don't know that he ever did that), but Paul's first prayer for these Ephesians is recorded in his little epistle to them: "Wherefore I also, after I heard of your faith in the Lord Jesus, and love unto all the saints, Cease not to give thanks for you, making mention of you in my prayers" (Eph. 1:15–16). Now what would Paul pray for? Here it is: "That the God of our Lord Jesus Christ, the Father of glory, may give unto you the spirit of wisdom and revelation in the knowledge of him: The eyes of your understanding being enlightened; that ye may know what is the hope of his calling, and what the riches of the glory of his inheritance in the saints" (Eph. 1:17–18). Paul's prayer, you see, is that they might have a wisdom and an understanding of the revelation of the knowledge of Him—that is, that they might know the Word of God. And that the eyes of their understanding might be enlightened, that they might know something of the hope of the calling they had in Christ. This is the prayer of the apostle Paul. And if anyone remembers me in prayer, this is exactly what I want them to pray for—that my eyes (my spiritual eyes) might be open. I believe the most important thing for you and me today is to know the will of God—and the will of God is the Word of God. We cannot know the Word of God unless the Spirit of God is our teacher. That is what Paul says over in the first epistle to the Corinthians: "Now we have received, not the spirit of the world, but the Spirit who is of God; that we might know the things that are freely given to us of God. Which things also we speak, not in the word which man's wisdom teacheth, but which the Holy Spirit teacheth, comparing spiritual things with spiritual. But the natural man receiveth not the things of the Spirit of God; for they are foolishness unto him, neither can he know them, because they are spiritually discerned" (1 Cor. 2:12–14, New Scofield Reference Bible). The reason today that so many don't get anything out of the Bible is simply because they are not letting the Spirit of God teach them. The Word of God is different from any other book, you see, because the natural man cannot receive these things. To him they are foolishness. God has given to us the Spirit that we might know the things that are freely given to us of God. He alone is our Teacher; He alone can take the Word of God and make it real and living to us.

God *wants* to communicate with us through His written Word. But it is a supernatural Book, and it will not communicate to us on the natural plane for the very simple reason that only the Spirit of God can take the things of Christ and reveal them to us. Notice this very interesting verse of Scripture: "For what man knoweth the things of a man, except the spirit of man which is in him? Even so the things of God knoweth no man, but the Spirit of God" (1 Cor. 2:11, New Scofield Reference Bible). In a very succinct and understandable manner, this gives the reason the Spirit of God must be our Teacher. You and I understand each other, but we do not understand God. I believe it is perfect nonsense to talk about a generation gap through which we cannot communicate. While it has always been true that it is difficult for an older person and a younger person to see eye to eye, we can communicate with each other because we are all human beings. We understand each other. But frankly, I don't understand God unless He is revealed to me. I used to wonder how He would feel at a funeral. Well, I find the Lord Jesus there at the funeral of Lazarus and see that He wept. I know how He feels today. I know how He feels about many things because the Spirit of God through the Word of God has revealed them to me.

When I was pastor in Nashville, Tennessee, I got up one bright morning and looked out my window. During the night about five inches of snow had fallen and covered up all the ugliness with a beautiful blanket. I sat upstairs in my study looking out over the scene when I noticed an elder of my church, who lived next door, come out on his porch with two coal scuttles filled with ashes which he was going to empty in the alley. I saw him stop and look over the landscape, and I just smiled because I knew how he felt—just like I felt, looking out on that snow that had fallen during the night. But when he started down the steps, he slipped. Not wanting to spill the ashes, he held them out and hit one of those steps with a real bump. I couldn't help but laugh. I guess if he had broken his neck I still would have laughed. But I noticed that he looked around, and when he was satisfied that nobody had seen him, he got up with great satisfaction and started out again. About halfway out on the sidewalk we had a repeat performance; only this time he fell much farther because he fell all the way to the sidewalk. And it looked to me like he bounced when he hit. This time he really scanned the landscape. He didn't want anybody to see what he had done. And I knew how he felt. I would have felt the same way. He got up and looked over the landscape, went out and emptied his ashes, and when he got back to the porch, he looked over the landscape again—I don't think this time to admire the scene but to make good and sure that no one had seen him fall. I didn't say a word until Sunday morning. When I came into the church, I went right by where he sat, leaned down and said, "You sure did look funny yesterday carrying out the ashes!"

He looked at me in amazement. He said, "Did you see me?"

I said, "Yes."

"Well," he said, "I didn't think anybody saw me."

And I said, "I thought that. I knew exactly how you felt." You see, he had a human spirit and I had a human spirit—we understood each other. But who can understand God? Only the Spirit of God. And that is the reason the Holy Spirit teaches us, comparing spiritual things with spiritual.

Renan, the French skeptic, made an attack on the Word of God; yet he wrote *Life of Jesus*. His book is divided into two sections, one is the historical section, the other is the interpretation of the life of Christ. As far as the first part is concerned, there probably has never been a more brilliant life of Christ written by any man. But his interpretation of it is positively absurd. It could have been done better by a twelve-year-old Sunday school boy. What is the explanation of that? Well, the Spirit of God does not teach you history or give you facts that you can dig out for yourself; a very clever mind can dig out those. But the interpretation is altogether different. The Spirit of God has to do the interpreting, and He alone must be the Teacher to lead us and guide us into all truth. We must have the Spirit of God to open our eyes to see.

And we are told to ask His help. In John 16 the Lord Jesus says, "I have yet many things to say unto you, but ye cannot bear them now. Howbeit when he, the Spirit of truth, is come, he will guide you into all truth: for he shall not speak of himself; but whatsoever he shall hear, that shall he speak: and he will shew you things to come. He shall glorify me: for he shall receive of mine, and shall shew it unto you. All things that the Father hath are mine; therefore said I, that he shall take of mine, and shall shew it unto you. A little while, and ye shall not see me: and again, a little while, and ye shall see me, because I go to the Father" (John 16:12–16). So the Lord Jesus is saying that we are to ask. He has many things for us, and He has sent the Holy Spirit to be the Teacher. Again in chapter 14 He says, "But the Comforter, which is the Holy Ghost, whom the Father will send in my name, he shall teach you all things, and bring all things to your remembrance, whatsoever I have said unto you" (John 14:26). The Holy Spirit is the Teacher, and He must be the One to lead us and guide us into all truth, friend. If you ever learn anything through my Bible study program, it will not be because this poor preacher is the teacher, it will be because the Spirit of God is opening up the Word of God to you.

This, then, is the first guideline: Begin with prayer and ask the Spirit of God to be your Teacher.

2. Read the Bible.

The second guideline may seem oversimplified.

Someone asked a great Shakespearean scholar years ago, "How do you study Shakespeare?" His answer was very terse, "Read Shakespeare." And I would say to you: Read the Word of God. Do you want to know what the Bible has to say? Read the Bible. Over and above what any teacher may give you, it is all-important to read for yourself what the Bible has to say.

Dr. G. Campbell Morgan has written some very wonderful and helpful commentaries on the Bible. In fact, he has a series of books that I recommend on all sixty-six books of the Bible. I know of nothing that is any better than them, and when I started out as a student, they had a great influence on my study of the Word. It is said that he would not put pen to paper until he had read a particular book of the Bible through fifty times. So don't be weary in well doing, friend; just read the Word of God. If you don't get it the first time, read it the second time. If you don't get it the second time, read it the third time. Keep on reading it. We are to get the facts of the Word of God.

There is a very interesting incident in the Book of Nehemiah: "And all the people gathered themselves together as one man into the street that was before the water gate; and they spake unto Ezra the scribe to bring the book of the law of Moses, which the LORD had commanded to Israel. And Ezra the priest brought the law before the congregation both of men and women, and all that could hear with understanding, upon the first day of the seventh month. And he read therein before the street that was before the water gate from the morning until mid-day, before the men and the women, and those who could understand; and the ears of all the people were attentive unto the book of the law" (Neh. 8:1–3). This is a very remarkable passage of Scripture. You see, the Jews had been in Babylonian captivity seventy years; many of them had never heard the Word of God. It did not circulate much in that day. There were not a hundred different translations abroad nor new ones coming off the press all the time. Probably there were just one or two copies in existence, and Ezra had one of those copies. He stood and read before the water gate. "So they read in the book in the law of God distinctly, and gave the sense, and caused them to understand the reading" (Neh. 8:8). From the way the account is given, I assume that men of the tribe of Levi were stationed in certain areas among the people. After Ezra had read a certain portion, he would stop to give the people who had listened an opportunity to ask questions of the men who were stationed out there to explain the Bible to them. ". . . and the Levites, caused the people to understand the law: and the people stood in their place" (Neh. 8:7). Not only did they read the Word, but they caused the people to understand it.

We need to read the Bible.

There are so many distractions today from the study of the Word of God. And the greatest distraction we have is the church. The church is made up of committees and organizations and banquets and entertainments and promotional schemes to the extent that the Word of God is not even dealt with in many churches today. There are churches that have disbanded the preaching service altogether. Instead they have a time in which the people will be able to express themselves and say what they are thinking. I can't imagine anything more puerile or more of a waste of time than that (although it is a fine excuse to get out of preaching for a lazy preacher who will not read or study the Bible.) I find that the people who are more ignorant of the Bible than anyone else are church members. They simply do not know the Word of God. And it has been years since it has been taught in the average church. We need to read the Bible. We need to get into the Word of God—not just reading a few favorite verses, but reading the *entire* Word of God. That is the only way we are going to know it, friend. That is God's method.

WHEN YOU READ THE BIBLE THROUGH

> *I supposed I knew my Bible,*
> *Reading piecemeal, hit or miss,*
> *Now a bit of John or Matthew,*
> *Now a snatch of Genesis,*

> Certain chapters of Isaiah,
> Certain Psalms (the twenty-third),
> Twelfth of Romans, First of Proverbs—
> Yes, I thought I knew the Word!
> But I found that thorough reading
> Was a different thing to do,
> And the way was unfamiliar
> When I read the Bible through.
> You who like to play at Bible,
> Dip and dabble, here and there,
> Just before you kneel, aweary,
> And yawn through a hurried prayer;
> You who treat the Crown of Writings
> As you treat no other book—
> Just a paragraph disjointed,
> Just a crude impatient look—
> Try a worthier procedure,
> Try a broad and steady view;
> You will kneel in very rapture
> When you read the Bible through!
> —Amos R. Wells

3. Study the Bible.

Someone came to Dr. G. Campbell Morgan, years ago, and said, "You speak as though you are inspired!" Dr. Morgan replied, "Inspiration is 95 percent perspiration." The Bible needs to be studied. We need to realize that the Spirit of God will not teach us something that we could get ourselves by study. I used to teach in a Bible institute, and the classes were made up of all kinds of young folk. Among them were a few very pious individuals, and I understood these young people very well after a period of time—I confess I didn't understand them at first. Their pious façade, I found, covered up tremendous ignorance and a vacuum relative to the Word of God. Some of them would not study the night before an exam. They always would give an excuse that they were busy in a prayer meeting or a service somewhere. I had the feeling that some of them believed that they could put their Bibles under their pillows at night and as they slept, the names of the kings of Israel and Judah would come up through the duck feathers! Believe me, it won't come up through the duck feathers. We have to knuckle down and study the Word of God. A fellow student in a Bible class when I was in college said, "Doctor, you have assigned us a section that is very dry." The professor, without even missing a step, said to him, "Then dampen it a little with sweat from your brow." The Bible should be studied, and it is very important we see that. There is a certain knowledge that the Spirit of God is not going to give you. I do not think He is revealing truth to lazy people. After all, you never learn logarithms or geometry or Greek by just reading a chapter of it just before you go to sleep at night!

Now you may be shocked when I say that I do not encourage devotional reading of the Bible. But over a period of years I have learned that a great many people who are very faithful in what they call devotional reading are very ignorant of the Bible. I stayed with a family for over a week when I was holding meetings in a place in middle Tennessee. Every morning at the breakfast table we had devotions. Unfortunately, breakfast was always a little late, and Susie and Willie were rushing to get away to school. I am confident that they didn't even know what was read. Dad was wanting to get away to work, and he generally made the Bible reading very brief. Always he'd say, "Well, I'll read this familiar passage this morning because we don't have much time." And, believe me, we didn't. By the time the reading was over, Susie and Willie left the table like they were shot out of a gun, Dad got out of there almost as quickly as they did, and Mother was left with the dishes—and I wondered if she had really heard what had been read. I determined right there and then that in my home we wouldn't have devotional reading. I have always encouraged members of my family to read the Bible on their own. That is the reading that is profitable.

Someone is going to say, "But I have my devotions at night after the day is over." Now really, don't you have them right before you go to bed? You've got one foot in bed already, one eye is already closed, and you turn to a passage of Scripture to read. You cannot learn mathematics that way. You cannot learn literature that way. And you cannot learn the *Bible* that way. You have to *study* the Word of God. You ought to read it when you can give time to it. And if you can't find time, you ought to *make* time. Set apart thirty minutes or an hour. Or if you do things haphazardly like I do, read thirty minutes one day, perhaps only five minutes the next day, and two or three hours the next day, however it fits into your program. I put down no particular rule except that each person should read for himself, and boys and girls should be encouraged to read the Bible for themselves. Some folk feel that they ought to have devotional reading together. And that is fine, if the Lord leads you to do it, but I guarantee you will not be intelligent Bible students after twenty years of doing it like that. You also need to study the Word of God on your own.

It was said of John Wesley that he was a man of one Book. What made him a man of one Book? Well, he got up and read the Bible at four and five o'clock every morning—read it in five different languages. Believe me, he studied the Word of God. And you and I need to study the Word; we need to get the meaning of the Bible.

4. Meditate on the Bible.

Meditation is something that God taught His people. The Word of God was to be before the children of Israel all the time—so that they could meditate on it. "And these words, which I command thee this day, shall be in thine heart: And thou shalt teach them diligently unto thy children, and shalt talk of them when thou sittest in thine house, and when thou walkest by the way, and when thou liest down, and when thou risest up. And thou shalt bind them for a sign upon thine hand, and they shall be as frontlets between thine eyes. And thou shalt write them upon the posts of thy house, and on thy gates" (Deut. 6:6–9). Now that is an amazing statement coming from the Lord. He told them to write the Word of God upon the doorposts. In other words, wherever they turned, it was just like looking at billboards. You cannot drive up and down our streets and highways without seeing liquor signs and cigarette signs—billboards galore! Now you can understand why people today drink liquor and why they smoke cigarettes—it is before them all the time. The Lord knew human nature. He knew us. And He told His people to get the Word where they would see it. It was on their doorposts, on their gates, and they wore it on their garments. And they were to talk about it when they were walking. They were to talk about the Word when they sat down. They were to talk about it when they went to bed and until they went to sleep. God asked His people to meditate on His Word.

Now what does it really mean to meditate on the Word of God? There is a very interesting statement over in the first Psalm: "Blessed is the man that walketh not in the counsel of the ungodly, nor standeth in the way of sinners, nor sitteth in the seat of the scornful. But his delight is in the law of the LORD; and in his law doth he meditate day and night" (Ps. 1:1–2). To meditate is to ruminate, to bring to mind, and to consider over and over. Ruminating is what a cow is doing when she is chewing her cud. You know how the old cow goes out in the morning, and while the grass is fresh with dew she grazes. Then when the sun comes up and the weather is hot, the cow lies down under a tree, or stands there in the shade. You see her chewing and you wonder what in the world that cow is chewing. She will chew there for an hour or two. Well, she is meditating, friend. She is bringing the grass she ate in the morning (we are told that a cow has a complex stomach) out of one chamber and is transferring it to another. In the process she is going over it again, chewing it up good. You and I need to learn to do that in our thought processes. We are to get the Word of God, read it, have it out where we can look at it, then think about it, meditate on it.

Many times in preparing a message I'll take a verse of Scripture and spend hours doing nothing but reading it over and over, checking what others have said about it, and just keep reading it. Finally new truth will break out from that particular passage. I remember hearing Dr. Harry Ironside say that he had heard a lecture on the Song of Solomon which left him dissatisfied. He said that he read the Song of Solomon again, got down on his knees and asked God to give him an understanding of it. He did that again and again—in fact, he did it for weeks and months. Finally new light broke from that book. When I teach the Song of Solomon I generally give Dr. Ironside's interpretation for two reasons: it satisfies my own mind and heart more than does any other interpretation I have heard, and I know the man who got it had spent a great deal of time in meditation.

There are folk who write to us saying that the wife listens to our Bible study by radio at home, and the husband listens to it at work, and at the dinner table they discuss the Scripture that was covered. That is meditation; it is going back over it again. Riding along in the car alone is a good place to take a passage of Scripture and really give thought to it.

How many of you, after you have had "devotions," meditate upon that passage during the day? Most people read it and then forget it—never thinking about it again until it is called to their attention. Or, if they read it at night, they jump into bed as quickly as they can, turn out the light, and go to sleep, forgetting all about it. Meditation is almost a lost art in our contemporary society. Frankly, television in many homes absolutely blots out the possibility for meditation. It is changing the spiritual life of many families today. One of the reasons that our churches are becoming colder and more indifferent to the Word of God is simply because there is that lack of meditation upon the Word of God.

Remember the Ethiopian eunuch who was riding along reading Isaiah (Acts 8). He was actually studying Isaiah, because he was in a passage with which he was having trouble—he did not know what it meant. Here is a man who is reading and studying, and the Spirit of God is going to open the Word of God to him. That is the reason the Holy Spirit brought Philip there to explain the chapter to the Ethiopian. It opened up a new world to him, and he came to know Christ. The record says that he went on his way rejoicing. What was making him rejoice? He was meditating. He was going back over that fifty-third chapter of Isaiah.

Have you ever meditated on that Lamb who was brought as a sheep to the slaughter? Who was He? He came from heaven and identified Himself with us who like sheep have gone astray and have turned every one to our own way. And the Lord has laid on Him the iniquity of us all. Do you meditate on these things? The Ethiopian did. It always has been a matter of speculation as to what he did after that. Tradition says that he went back to his land and founded the Coptic church of Ethiopia. That could well be; we do not know. However, the interesting thing is that he went on his way rejoicing, which lets us know that he was meditating on the Word of God.

5. Read What Others Have Written on the Scriptures.

I know that this is a dangerous rule, because many folk depend on what someone else says about the Bible. Also there are many books on the market today that give wrong teaching concerning the Word of God. We need to test everything that is written by the Bible itself.

However, you and I should consult a good commentary. With each outline of the books of the Bible I list recommended books, commentaries that I have read and have found helpful. You will find it very profitable to read what others have said. Actually, you are getting all the distilled sweetness and study of the centuries when you read books written by men who have been guided in their study by the Spirit of God. You and I should profit by this. There have been some wonderful, profound works on the books of the Bible.

In addition to commentaries, a concordance is invaluable. I can recommend three: Young's concordance, Strong's concordance, and Cruden's concordance—take your pick. Also you will need a good Bible dictionary. The *Davis Bible Dictionary* is good if you don't get the wrong edition. *Unger's Bible Dictionary* I can recommend without reservation.

Every teacher and preacher of the gospel has a set of books that he studies. He needs them. Someone asks, "Should he present verbatim what somebody else has written?" No, he should never do that, unless he gives credit to the author. But he has a perfect right to use what others have written. I have been told that some of my feeble messages are given by others, and sometimes credit is given and sometimes no mention is made of the author at all. As far as I'm personally concerned, it makes no difference, but it does reveal the character of the individual who will use someone else's material verbatim and not give credit for it. A professor in seminary solved this problem. When someone asked him if he should quote other writers, he said, "You ought to graze on everybody's pasture, but give your own milk." And that means that you are to read what others have written, but you put it in your own thought patterns and express it your way. You have a perfect right to do that. The important thing is that we should take advantage of the study of other men in the Word of God.

6. Obey the Bible.

For the understanding and the study of the Scriptures, *obedience* is essential. Abraham is an example of this. God appeared to him when He called him out of Ur of the Chaldees and again when he was in the Promised Land. But Abraham ran off to Egypt when famine came, and during this time God had no word for him. Not until Abraham was back in the land did God appear to him again. Why? Because of lack of obedience. Until Abraham obeyed what God had already revealed to him, God was not prepared to give to him any new truth. So it is with us. When we obey, God opens up new truth for us.

Even the gospel which is given to save our souls is given for the very definite purpose of obedience. The greatest document that ever has been written on the gospel is the Epistle to the Romans. And Paul put around the gospel this matter of obedience. He begins with it: "By whom we have received grace and apostleship, for obedience to the faith among all nations, for his name" (Rom. 1:5). Again at the end of Romans, Paul comes back to this: "But now is made manifest, and by the scriptures of the prophets, according to the commandment of the everlasting God, made known to all nations for the obedience of faith" (Rom. 16:26). "Obedience of faith" is the last thing Paul says in this epistle. What is between? He sets before us what the gospel is, that great doctrinal section; then he concludes with a section on duty—what we're to do. Paul put around the gospel this matter of obedience.

Obedience to the faith. This is where Adam and Eve went wrong. She not only listened to Satan, the enemy of God, but she also disobeyed God.

Obedience to God is very important. And we must recognize that God will not continue to reveal truth to us if we become disobedient. We must obey the Bible if we are to profit from its reading.

Also obedience is important because there are folk who measure Christianity by you and by me. Cowan has well said, "The best way to defend the Gospel is to live a life worthy of the Gospel." That is the way you prove it is the Word of God.

Four clergymen were discussing the merits of various translations of the Bible. One liked the King James Version best because of its simple, beautiful English. Another liked the American Standard Version because it is more literal and comes nearer to the Hebrew and Greek texts. Still another liked a modern translation because of its up-to-date vocabulary. The fourth minister was silent. When asked to express his opinion, he replied, "I like my mother's translation best. She translated it into life, and it was the most convincing translation I have ever seen."

You will recall that Paul wrote to the Corinthian Christians: "Ye are our epistle written in our hearts, known and read of all men: Forasmuch as ye are manifestly declared to be the epistle of Christ ministered by us, written not with ink, but with the Spirit of the living God; not in tables of stone, but in fleshy tables of the heart" (2 Cor. 3:2–3).

> The Gospel is written a chapter a day
> By deeds that you do and words that you say.
> Men read what you say whether faithless or true.
> Say, what is the Gospel according to you?
> —Author Unknown

That little jingle is true. Oh, how important it is to obey the Bible! I believe that today Christianity is being hurt more by those who are church members than by any other group. That is one of the reasons that we have all of this rebellion on the outside—rebellion against the establishment, which includes the church. A placard carried by one in a protest march had four words on it: "Church no; Jesus, yes." Candidly, the lives of a great many in the church are turning people away from the church. A barrister in England years ago was asked why he did not become a Christian. This was his answer: "I, too, might have become a Christian if I had not met so many who said they were Christians." How unfortunate that is! We need to examine our own lives in this connection. How important it is to *obey* the Word of God!

7. Pass It On to Others.

Not only read the Bible, not only study the Bible, not only meditate on the Bible, and not only read what others have written about it, but pass it on to others. That is what we all should do. You will reach a saturation point in the study of the Word unless you do share it with others. God won't let you withdraw yourself from mankind and become some sort of a walking Bible encyclopedia, knowing everything, while the rest of us remain ignorant. I think that is the reason He said: "Not forsaking the assembling of ourselves together, as the manner of some is; but exhorting one another: and so much the more, as ye see the day approaching" (Heb. 10:25).

God has told us to be witnesses. He said, "Ye shall be witnesses" (Acts 1:8). He did not say that we should be scholars, walking encyclopedias, or memory books. He did not say we should bury God's truth in a notebook. Someone has said that education is a process by which information in the professor's notebook is transferred to the student's notebook, without passing through the mind of either. Well, there is a great deal of Bible truth like that. It is not practiced, not shared. We are called to be witnesses today, therefore we ought to pass it on to others.

I learned this lesson when I was in seminary. I pastored a little church, as did five other fellows, and we found that when we were graduated, we were at least a year ahead of the other members of the class. Why? Because we were smarter than the others? No. Because we were passing it on. God was able to funnel into us a great deal more than He might have otherwise.

My friend, pass it on.

These, then, are the seven basic guidelines to follow as you take in your hands the Word of God:

1. Begin with prayer.
2. Read the Bible.
3. Study the Bible.
4. Meditate on the Bible.
5. Read what others have written on the Bible.
6. Obey the Bible.
7. Pass it on to others.

The Book of
GENESIS

INTRODUCTION

The Book of Genesis is one of the two important key books of the Bible. The book that opens the Old Testament (Genesis) and the book that opens the New Testament (Matthew) are the two books which I feel are the key to the understanding of the Scriptures.

Before beginning this study, I would like to suggest that you read the Book of Genesis through. It would be preferable to read it at one sitting. I recognize that this may be impossible for you to do, and if you want to know the truth, I have not been able to do it in one sitting. It has taken me several sittings because of interruptions. However, if you find it possible to read through Genesis at one sitting, you will find it very profitable.

Let me give you a bird's-eye view of Genesis, a view that will cover the total spectrum of the book. There are certain things that you should note because the Book of Genesis is, actually, germane to the entire Scripture. The fact of the matter is that Genesis is a book that states many things for the first time: creation, man, woman, sin, sabbath, marriage, family, labor, civilization, culture, murder, sacrifice, races, languages, redemption, and cities.

You will also find certain phrases that occur very frequently. For instance, "these are the generations of" is an important expression used frequently because the Book of Genesis gives the families of early history. That is important to us because we are members of the human family that begins here.

A number of very interesting characters are portrayed for us. Someone has called this "the book of biographies." There are Abraham, Isaac, Jacob, Joseph, Pharaoh, and the eleven sons of Jacob besides Joseph. You will find that God is continually blessing Abraham, Isaac, Jacob, and Joseph. In addition, those who are associated with them—Lot, Abimelech, Potiphar, the butler, and Pharaoh—are also blessed of God.

In this book you will find mention of the covenant. There are frequent appearances of the Lord to the patriarchs, especially to Abraham. The altar is prominent in this book. Jealousy in the home is found here. Egypt comes before us in this book as it does nowhere else. The judgments upon sin are mentioned here, and there are evident leadings of Providence.

As we study, we need to keep in mind something that Browning wrote years ago in a grammarian's funeral essay: "Image the whole, then execute the parts. Fancy the fabric, quiet, e'er you build, e'er steel strike fire from quartz, e'er mortar dab brick." In other words, get the total picture of this book. I tell students that there are two ways of studying the Bible; one is with the telescope and the other way is with the microscope. At first, you need to get the telescopic view. After that, study it with a microscope.

A great preacher of the past, Robinson of England, has written something which I would like to write indelibly on the minds and hearts of God's people today:

> We live in the age of books. They pour out for us from the press in an ever increasing multitude. And we are always reading manuals, textbooks, articles, books of devotion, books of criticism, books about the Bible, books about the Gospels, all are devoured with avidity. But what amount of time and labor do we give to the consideration of the Gospels themselves? We're constantly tempted to imagine that we get good more quickly by reading some modern statement of truth which we find comparatively easy to appropriate because it is presented to us in a shape, and from a standpoint, with which our education, or it may be partly association, has made us familiar. But the good we acquire readily is not that which enters most deeply into our being and becomes an abiding possession. It would be well if

we could realize quite simply that nothing worth the having is to be gained without the winning. The great truths of nature are not offered to us in such a form as to make it easy to grasp them. The treasures of grace must be sought with all the skill and energy which are characteristic of the man who is searching for goodly pearls. (Robinson, *The Personal Life of the Clergy*.)

I love that statement because I believe that the Bible itself will speak to our hearts in a way that no other book can do. Therefore we have included the text of Scripture in this study. New translations are appearing in our day; in fact, they are coming from the presses as fast and prolifically as rabbits multiply. However, I will continue to use the Authorized or King James Version. I refuse to substitute the pungency of genius with the bland, colorless, and tasteless mediocrity of the present day.

MAJOR DIVISIONS OF THE BOOK

Where would you divide the Book of Genesis if you divided it into two parts? Notice that the first eleven chapters constitute a whole and that, beginning with chapter 12 through the remainder of the book, we find an altogether different section. The two parts differ in several ways: The first section extends from creation to Abraham. The second section extends from Abraham through Joseph. The first section deals with major *subjects*, subjects which still engage the minds of thoughtful men in our day: the Creation, the Fall, the Flood, the Tower of Babel. The second section has to do with personalities: Abraham, the man of faith; Isaac, the beloved son; Jacob, the chosen and chastened son; and Joseph, his suffering and glory.

Although that is a major division, there is another division even more significant. It has to do with *time*. The first eleven chapters cover a minimum time span of two thousand years—actually, two thousand years *plus*. I feel that it is safe to say that they may cover several hundred thousand years. I believe this first section of Genesis can cover any time in the past that you may need to fit into your particular theory, and the chances are that you would come short of it even then. At least we know the book covers a minimum of two thousand years in the first eleven chapters, but the second section of thirty-nine chapters covers only three hundred and fifty years. In fact, beginning with Genesis 12 and running all the way through the Old Testament and the New Testament, a total time span of only two thousand years is covered. Therefore, as far as *time* is concerned, you are halfway through the Bible when you cover the first eleven chapters of Genesis.

This should suggest to your mind and heart that God had some definite purpose in giving this first section to us. Do you think that God is putting the emphasis on this first section or on the rest of the Bible? Isn't it evident that He is putting the emphasis on the last part? The first section has to do with the universe and with creation, but the last part deals with man, with nations, and with the person of Jesus Christ. God was more interested in Abraham than He was in the entire created universe. And, my friend, God is more interested in you and attaches more value to you than He does to the entire physical universe.

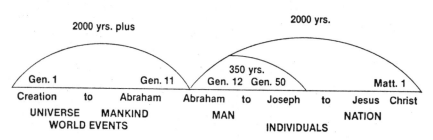

Let me further illustrate this. Of the eighty-nine chapters in the four Gospel records, only four chapters cover the first thirty years of the life of the Lord Jesus while eighty-five chapters cover the last three years of His life, and twenty-seven chapters cover the final eight *days* of His life. Where does that indicate that the Spirit of God is placing the emphasis? I am sure you will agree that the emphasis is on the last part, the last eight days covered by the twenty-seven chapters. And what is that all about? It's about the death, burial, and resurrection of the Lord Jesus Christ. That is the important part of the Gospel record. In other words, God has given the Gospels that you might believe that Christ died for our sins and that He was raised for our justification. That is essential. That is the all-important truth.

May I say that the first eleven chapters of Genesis are merely the introduction to the Bible, and we need to look at them in this fashion. This does not mean that we are going to pass over the first eleven chapters. Actually, we will spend quite a bit of time with them.

Genesis is the "seed plot" of the Bible, and here we find the beginning, the source, the birth of everything. The Book of Genesis is just like the bud of a beautiful rose, and it opens out into the rest of the Bible. The truth here is in germ form.

One of the best divisions which can be made of the Book of Genesis is according to the genealogies—i.e., according to the families.

Gen. 1—2:6	Book of Generations of Heavens and Earth
Gen. 2:7—6:8	Book of Generations of Adam
Gen. 6:9—9:29	Generations of Noah
Gen. 10:1—11:9	Generations of Sons of Noah
Gen. 11:10–26	Generations of Sons of Shem
Gen. 11:27—25:11	Generations of Terah
Gen. 25:12–18	Generations of Ishmael
Gen. 25:19—35:29	Generations of Isaac
Gen. 36:1—37:1	Generations of Esau
Gen. 37:2—50:26	Generations of Jacob

All of these are given to us in the Book of Genesis. It is a book of families. Genesis is an amazing book, and it will help us to look at it from this viewpoint.

OUTLINE

I. **Entrance of Sin on Earth, Chapters 1—11**
  A. Creation, Chapters 1 and 2
    1. Heaven and Earth, 1:1
      "Create" (bara) occurs only 3 times, vv. 1, 21, 27
    2. Earth Became Waste and Void, 1:2
    3. Re-creation, 1:3—2:25
      (a) First Day—Light, 1:3–5
      (b) Second Day—Air Spaces (Firmament), 1:6–8
      (c) Third Day—
         Dry Land Appears and Plant Life, 1:9–13
      (d) Fourth Day—Sun, Moon, Stars Appear, 1:14–19
      (e) Fifth Day—Animal Life (Biology), 1:20–23
      (f) Sixth Day—
         Fertility of Creation and Creation of Man, 1:24–31
      (g) Seventh Day—Sabbath, 2:1–3
      (h) Recapitulation of the Creation of Man, 2:4–25
         (Law of recurrence)

  B. Fall, Chapters 3 and 4
    1. Root of Sin—Doubting and Disobeying God
    2. Fruit of Sin—
      "Out of the heart proceed . . . murders . . ."
      (Matt. 15:19)

  C. Flood (Deluge), Chapters 5—9
    1. Book of Generations of Adam—Through Seth
      Beginning of Man's History—
      Obituary Notices, Chapter 5
    2. Antediluvian Civilization—
      Cause of Flood and Construction of Ark, Chapter 6
    3. Judgment of Flood, Chapter 7
    4. Postdiluvian Civilization—
      After the Flood, Chapter 8

(c) Jacob Sends Sons (Benjamin Included) Again to Egypt—
Joseph Entertains Brothers (Does Not Reveal His Identity), Chapter 43

(d) Joseph Sends Brothers Home—
Arrested by Steward—
Cup Found in Benjamin's Sack—
Judah Pleads for Benjamin, Chapter 44

(e) Joseph Reveals Identity—
Tender Reunion with Brothers—
Invites Jacob and All Family to Egypt, Chapter 45

(f) Jacob with Family (70) Moves to Egypt—
Jacob and Joseph Reunited, Chapter 46

(g) Jacob and Brothers Dwell in Goshen—
Presented to Pharaoh—
Famine Forces Egyptians to Sell Land to Joseph for Pharaoh—
Joseph Swears He Will Bury Jacob in Canaan, Chapter 47

(h) Jacob on Deathbed Blesses Joseph's Sons, Chapter 48

5. Death and Burial of Jacob and Joseph, Chapters 49 and 50

(a) Jacob Gives Deathbed Blessing and Prophecy for Twelve Sons, Chapter 49

(b) Death of Jacob and Burial in Canaan—
Death and Burial of Joseph in Egypt, Chapter 50

CHAPTER 1

THEME: Creation of the universe; construction of the
earth; day one—light; day two—air spaces; day three
—dry land and plant life; day four—sun, moon, and
stars appear; day five—animal life; day six—fertility
of animal life; creation of man

CREATION OF THE UNIVERSE

**In the beginning God created the heaven and the earth
[Gen. 1:1].**

This is one of the most profound statements that has ever been
made, and yet we find that it is a statement that is certainly chal-
lenged in this hour in which we are living. I think that this verse is all
we have of the actual creation—with the exception, as we shall see,
of the creation of man and animals later on in the Book of Genesis.
But this is the creation story, and I'll admit that it is a very brief story,
indeed.

An incident was told by Paul Bellamy, the late city editor of the
Cleveland Plain Dealer, that while he was making the rounds of the
reporters' desks one night, he noticed one of his men grinding out a
"tapeworm" on what Bellamy regarded as a relatively unimportant
event. "Cut it down!" he said. "After all, the story of the creation was
told in Genesis in 282 words." The reporter shot back, "Yes, and I've
always thought we could have been saved a lot of arguments later if
someone had just written another couple hundred."

It is interesting to note that God certainly has given us an abridged
edition. The question arises: What did He have in mind when He gave
us this particular section? What was the Author's purpose here? Was it
His purpose to teach geology? There is a great deal of argument and
disagreement at this particular juncture. Sometime ago here in California, the state board of education voted to include the biblical so-
called theory of creation in science books. Now frankly, I'm not so

sure that I'm happy about that. Someone will say that I ought to be because it is a step in the right direction. My friends, I'll tell you why I'm not happy. My concern is relative to the *character* of the teachers who teach it. We don't have enough teachers with a Christian background and with a Bible background to be able to teach it properly. Very few of the public school teachers are prepared, really, to teach the story of creation.

Dr. Ralph Girard, professor of biology and dean of the graduate division at the University of California at Davis is reported by the press to have made the comment that the "theory of creation" makes about as much sense as teaching about the stork. He asked if a scientific course on reproduction should also mention the stork theory. The very interesting thing is that the stork theory is not mentioned in the Bible at all, but the creation story is mentioned. His comparison is not quite warranted, because the Bible deals literally with this matter of procreation, and if you read your Bible carefully, you never could have the viewpoint of the stork theory! So what this man says is certainly beside the point but reveals a very antagonistic attitude toward the Bible. I'm of the opinion that this man probably knows a great deal about this particular subject, which seems to be biology, but he knows very little about the Word of God. This is quite obvious from the type of statement he has made.

This problem of origin provokes more violent controversy, wild theories, and wide disagreement than any other. Always there is the inclusion of men's hypotheses, and as a result there is a babble of voices that has drowned out the clear voice of God. Actually, there are two extreme groups who have blurred the issue, and they have muddied the waters of understanding by their dogmatic assumptions and assertions. One group is comprised of the arrogant scientists who assume that biological and philosophical evolution are the gospel truth. Their assumed axiom is "the assured finding of science," and we'll look into that in a moment. The other group is comprised of the young and proud theologians who arrogate to themselves the super-knowledge that they have discovered how God did it. They write and speak learnedly about some clever theory that reconciles science and the Bible. They look with disdain upon the great giants of biblical expositors of the past as being Bible dwarfs compared to them.

I would say that both of these groups would do well to consider a statement that was made to Job when the Lord finally appeared to him. God asked him the question: "Where wast thou when I laid the foundations of the earth? declare, if thou hast understanding" (Job 38:4). In other words, God is saying to man, "You talk about the origin of the universe, but you don't even know where *you* were when I laid the foundation of the earth!"

There are a great many theories as to how the world began, but all of them can be boiled down to fit into a twofold classification: one is creation, and the other is speculation. All theories fall into one of these two divisions.

The theory of evolution is comprised of many different theories in our day, and some of the most reputable scientists of the past, as well as of the present, reject evolution. So we can't put down the theory of evolution as being a scientific statement like $2 + 2 = 4$. Then there is the creation account in Genesis 1, which must be accepted by faith. It is very interesting that God has made it that way—by *faith* is the only way in the world by which you can accept it. Notice what the writer to the Hebrews said: "Now faith is the substance of things hoped for, the evidence of things not seen. For by it the elders obtained a good report. Through faith we understand that the worlds were framed by the word of God, so that things which are seen were not made of things which do appear" (Heb. 11:1–3). So today the great problem still remains. How did it get from nothing to something? The only way that you can ever arrive at an answer is by faith or by speculation—and speculation is very unscientific.

Now let us look at some of the theories of origin. There are those who tell us that we should accept the scientific answer. I would like to ask, what is the scientific answer? What science are we talking about? In the year 1806 Professor Lyell said that the French Institute enumerated not less than eighty geological theories which were hostile to the Scriptures, but not one of these theories is held in our day.

Moses is the human agent whom God used to write the book of

Genesis, and I think he would smile at all the disturbance today regarding the creation story because he did not write it with the intention of giving a scientific account. Paul tells us the purpose of all Scripture: "All scripture is given by inspiration of God, and is profitable for doctrine, for reproof, for correction, for instruction in righteousness: That the man of God may be perfect, throughly furnished unto all good works" (2 Tim. 3:16–17). The purpose of the Scripture is for instruction in righteousness. It was not written to teach you geology or biology. It was written to show man's relationship to God and God's requirements for man and what man must do to be saved. You can write this over the first part of the Book of Genesis: "What must I do to be saved?"

May I ask you, if God had given a scientific statement of creation, how many people of Moses' day could have understood it? How many people even in our day could grasp it? You must remember that the Bible was not written for only learned professors but also for simple folk of every age and in every land. If it had been written in the scientific language of Moses' time, it certainly would have been rejected.

Therefore, men have proposed several solutions relative to the origin of the universe. One is that it is an illusion. Well, that is certainly contrary to fact, is it not? And yet there are people who hold that theory. There are others who believe that it spontaneously arose out of nothing. (In a way, this is what the Bible states, although it goes further and says that God spoke it into existence; He created it.) Another view is that it had no origin but has existed eternally. A fourth view is that it was created, and this breaks down into many different theories which men hold in an attempt to explain the origin of the universe.

I have before me some of these theories which men have advanced down through the history of the world. Here is a statement by Dr. Harlow Shapely, the former director of the Harvard Observatory, who commented that we are still imbedded in abysmal ignorance of the world in which we live. He observed that "we have advanced very little, relative to the total surmisable extent of knowledge, beyond the level of wisdom acquired by animals of long racial experience. We are, to be sure, no longer afraid of strange squeaks in the dark, nor completely superstitious about the dead. On many occasions we are valantly rational. Nevertheless, we know how much the unknown transcends what we know." In other words, we are still absolutely in the dark relative to the origin of this earth on which we live.

Dr. Loren C. Eiseley, Office of the Provost, University of Pennsylvania, was asked about this; he answered that "we do not know any more about matter and how it is produced than we know about spiritual things. Therefore, I think it is unwise to say in our present state of knowledge that the one precludes the other. The universe seems to exist as a series of emergent levels, none of which is like the level below. That man and all the rest of life have evolved and changed is undeniable, but what lies beneath these exterior manifestations, we do not know. I wish I could answer your question, but to clothe my ignorance in big words would benefit neither yourself nor me."

One article says that man is on the verge of discovering the mystery of the origin of the world. That happened to be written back in 1961. We haven't had anything new on that since then, by the way.

The biologist Edwin Conklin, speaking of evolution, stated that the probability of life originating by accident is "comparable to the probability of the unabridged dictionary originating from an explosion in a print shop." That sounds very unscientific, coming from a scientist, but it's true.

There seem to be at least three theories of the origin of the universe which even astronomers have suggested, and it is interesting to note them. One is known as the "steady state" theory, one is the "big bang" theory, and another is the "oscillating" theory.

A Caltech scientist, Dr. William A. Baum, speaking at UCLA, told the National Academy of Science that new findings tend to rule out the "steady state" theory that the universe has always existed and that new matter is continually being created. Several years ago that was the accepted theory; now they have a new theory for the origin of the universe. Dr. Baum apparently held the "big bang" theory, which is that a great explosion took place billions of years ago and that we are in for another one in probably another ten billion years. I don't think we need to worry about that a great deal, but it is an interesting theory and one that was fathered in Great Britain.

Several years ago, Dr. Louis Leakey, an anthropologist (the son of a missionary, by the way) discovered in Africa what he called a missing link. He dug up pieces of a skull with well-developed teeth, called it the "nutcracker man" and claimed it belonged to a teenage youth about six hundred thousand years ago. Well, we have had theories like that before, and since we've heard no more of this one since 1961, I guess the scientific world didn't fall for it.

There are other ways for explaining the origin of man. Dr. Lawrence S. Dillon, associate professor of biology at Texas A and M College, says that man is not an animal but a plant which evolved from brown seaweed. Now maybe you have been looking in the wrong place for your grandpa and grandma. Some folk have been looking up a tree. Now we are told that we should be down at the beach pulling out seaweed because that is grandpa and grandma! Some of this speculation really becomes ridiculous.

A long time ago I read in a leading secular magazine that: "After centuries of bitter arguments over how life on earth began, an awe-inspiring answer is emerging out of the shrewd and patient detective work in laboratories all over the world." You would think that by now we would be getting some straight answers or at least a little encouragement, but none has been forthcoming.

It was the practice, according to J. V. N. Talmage, that the dogma which scientists followed was this: "The archaeological finds of prehistoric cultural objects must be so arranged that the cruder industries must always be dated earlier than those of a 'more advanced' type, regardless of where they are found." It has been a little disconcerting to find some of the advanced civilizations *underneath* those who seem to be of prehistoric time.

So many other theories are offered today about how the earth began. Dr. Klaus Mampell from Germany reportedly said that he didn't see any more reason for seeing us (the human race) connected with apes than with canary birds or kangaroos.

The evolutionary theory is divided up into many different phases and viewpoints. It has never been demonstrated as being true. It is unfortunate that when you get down to the level of the pseudo-scientists, and I'm thinking of the teachers today in our public schools who teach science, they really are not in a position to give a fair view because they were given only one viewpoint in college.

There is no unanimous acceptance of evolution even by scientists. Here is a quotation from Dr. G. A. Kerkut, of the Department of Physiology and Biochemistry at the University of Southampton in England. Though he himself is an evolutionist, in his book, *The Implications of Evolution,* he writes: "There is a theory which states that many living animals can be observed over the course of time to undergo changes so that new species are formed. This can be called the "Special Theory of Evolution" and can be demonstrated in certain cases by experiments. On the other hand there is the theory that all of the living forms in the world have arisen from a single source which itself came from an inorganic form. This theory can be called the "General Theory of Evolution" and the evidence that supports it is not sufficiently strong to allow us to consider it as anything more than a working hypothesis." Now listen to the statement of the Swedish botanist, Dr. Heribert Nilsson, who is also an evolutionist: "My attempts to demonstrate evolution by experiment carried on for more than forty years, have completely failed. . . . At least I should hardly be accused of having started from a preconceived antievolutionary standpoint. . . ." It may be firmly maintained that it is not even possible to make a caricature out of paleobiological facts. The fossil material is now so complete that it has been possible to construct new classes, and the lack of transitional series cannot be explained as due to the scarcity of material. Deficiencies are real. They will never be filled. . . . The idea of an evolution rests on pure belief."

May I say to you, he is moving into the realm of religion! My friend, to be an evolutionist you have to take it by *faith.* Evolution is speculation and always has been that. But, unfortunately, a great many folk have accepted it as fact.

In our day a group of theologians (young theologians for the most part) who, not wanting to be called intellectual obscurantists, have adopted what is known as "theistic evolution." If you would like to know what one scientist says about it, Kirtly Mather, in *Science Ponders Religion,* says: "When a theologian accepts evolution as the process used by the creator, he must be willing to go all the way with it. Not only is it an orderly process, it is a continuing one. The golden age for man—if any—is in the future, not in the past. . . . Moreover, the creative process of evolution is not to be interrupted by any supernatural intervention. The evolution of the first living cells from previously existing nonliving materials may represent a quantum jump rather than an infinitesimal step along the path of progress, but it is an entirely natural development." Theistic evolution is probably the most unrealistic of all theories. It is almost an unreasonable tenet and an illogical position. There are those today who are trying to run with the hare and with the hounds. They would like to move up with the unbelievers, but they also like to carry a Scofield Bible under their arm. My friend, it is difficult to do both. It is like that old Greek race in which a contestant rode with one foot on one horse and the other foot on another horse. It was marvelous when the two horses kept on the same route. But, believe me, when one of the horses decided to go in another direction, the rider had to determine which one he was going with. That is the condition of the theistic evolutionist. He ordinarily ends up riding the wrong horse, by the way.

In our day there is so much misinformation in the minds of intelligent human beings. For example, before me is a clipping from a secular magazine from several years ago. It posed a question, then answered it. First, the question: "What, according to biblical records, is the date of the creation of the world?" Now listen to the answer that was given: "4,004 B.C." How utterly ridiculous can one be?

An article in *Life* magazine concerning the origin of life said that at some indeterminate point—some say two billion years ago, some a billion and a half—life miraculously appeared on the surface of the deep. What form it took, science cannot specify. All that can be said, according to this article, is that "through some agency certain giant molecules acquired the ability to duplicate themselves." My friend, are you willing to go along with the theory that giant molecules acquired the ability to duplicate themselves?

Other ridiculous theories have been advanced. One is that man began on this earth from garbage that some prehistoric intelligence left on this earth in the dim and distant past. That statement comes from a *scientist!* While some scientists send us out to look for our ancestors in the trees, another sends us out to look at the seaweed, and now some send us to the garbage can! This is getting worse and worse, is it not? I don't know about you, but I feel that God's statement of creation still stands in this modern age.

A famous definition of evolution which Herbert Spencer gave stated that: "An integration of matter and concomitant dissipation of motion during which the matter passes from an indefinite, incoherent, homogeneity to a definite, coherent heterogeneity, and during which the retained motion undergoes a parallel transformation." You ponder that one for awhile, friend!

It still makes more sense to me to read: "In the beginning God created the heaven and the earth." Who created the universe? God did. He created it out of nothing. When? I don't know, and nobody else knows. Some men say one billion years ago, some say two billion, and now some say five billion. I personally suspect that they are all pikers. I think it was created long before that. My friend. we need to keep in mind that God has eternity behind Him. What ao you think He has been doing during all the billions of years of the past? Waiting for you and me to come on the scene? No, He has been busy. He has had this creation a long time to work with. You see, He really has not told us very much, has He? It is presumptuous of little man down here on earth to claim to know more than he really knows.

> You cannot put one little star in motion;
> You cannot shape one single forest leaf,
> Nor fling a mountain up, nor sink an ocean,
> Presumptuous pigmy, large with unbelief!
>
> You cannot bring one dawn of regal splendor,
> Nor bid the day to shadowy twilight fall,
> Nor send the pale moon forth with radiance tender;
> And dare you doubt the One who has done it all?
> —Sherman A. Nagel, Sr.

It behooves us to just accept that majestic statement which opens the Word of God: "In the beginning God created the heaven and the earth." And with the psalmist let us consider *His* heavens, the work of *His* fingers, the moon and the stars, which *He* hast ordained (Ps. 8:3) and realize that "the heavens declare the glory of God; and the firmament sheweth his handiwork" (Ps. 19:1).

The apostle Paul wrote this to the Romans: "For the invisible things of him from the creation of the world are clearly seen, being understood by the things that are made, even his eternal power and Godhead; so that they are without excuse" (Rom. 1:20). And the writer to the Hebrews says: "Through faith we understand that the worlds were framed by the word of God, so that things which are seen were not made of things which do appear" (Heb. 11:3). We must accept creation by faith. Even science cannot tell us how something can be made out of nothing. God apparently did it just that way. And man today cannot tell when this was created.

When we compare the Genesis record with other creation accounts, the contrasts are striking indeed. Most nations have a legend of creation, and probably all of them are corruptions of the Genesis account. For example, we find one of the best accounts of a secular nation in the Babylonian tablets of creation. Notice some of the contrasts: The Babylonian tablets begin with chaos. The Bible account begins with cosmos, with perfection. "In the beginning God created the heaven and the earth." According to the Babylonian account, the heavenly bodies are gods, but they are nothing in the world but matter according to the Bible. There is a polytheistic theology in the Babylonian account but a monotheistic truth in the Bible account. The Babylonian account says the universe is just the work of a craftsman, but the Bible says that God spoke and it came into existence. The Babylonian account is characterized by its puerility and grotesqueness, whereas the Bible presents grand and solemn realities of the Creator God who is holy and who is a Savior. The Babylonian account is definitely out of harmony with known science, but the Bible is in accord with true science.

I reject evolution because it rejects God and it rejects revelation. It denies the fall of man and the fact of sin, and it opposes the virgin birth of Christ. Therefore, I reject it with all my being. I do not believe that it is the answer to the origin of this universe.

There are three essential areas into which evolution cannot move and which evolution cannot solve. It cannot bridge the gap from nothing to something. It cannot bridge the gap from something to life. It cannot bridge the gap between life and humanity—that is, self-conscious human life with a free will.

The press, of course, is always looking for something sensational and comes up with interesting findings. One of the things which has been put in my hands is a clipping from a fellow Texan. They have found near Glenrose, Texas, down near a place where I used to live, the tracks of dinosaurs. Now, I've known about that for years. You might expect that in Texas they would find the biggest of everything, and apparently the dinosaurs were there. But now they have found something that is quite disturbing: they have found some giant human tracks in the same place. You know, that's really upsetting because it is very difficult to start out with a little amoeba or a little scum on top of the water and then find that walking back there with the dinosaurs were human beings who were much bigger than any of us today. Evolution is going to have a lot of problems in the next few years. May I predict (and I am merely echoing a prediction of a scientist) that by the end of this century the theory of evolution will be as dead as a dodo bird.

While there is a great deal more that could be said on these issues, there is a third question that arises. Not only are folk asking *who* created and *when* did He create but also *why* did He create. Believe me, this gets right down to the nitty-gritty. This is very important.

The Word of God tells us that this universe was created for His own pleasure. He saw fit to create it; He delighted in it. In the final book of the Bible we find these words: "Thou art worthy, O Lord, to receive glory and honour and power: for thou hast created all things, and for thy pleasure they are and were created" (Rev. 4:11). He created this universe because He wanted to create it. He did it for His pleasure. You may not like the universe, but He does. He never asked me about where I wanted this little world on which I live to be located in His universe. In fact, He didn't even ask me whether I wanted to be born in Texas or not. Of course, if He had given me the opportunity, I would have chosen Texas. But He didn't give me that choice. May I say to you that this universe was created for His pleasure. He saw fit to create and He delighted in the act.

The second reason that He created this universe was for His own glory. The original creation, you remember, sang that wonderful Creator's praise ". . . When the morning stars sang together, and all the sons of God shouted for joy" (Job 38:7). It was created for His glory. And in the prophecy of Isaiah are these words: ". . . I have created him for my glory, I have formed him; yea, I have made him" (Isa. 43:7). God created this universe for His own glory.

The Word of God also tells us that God created man in this universe for fellowship. He wanted to have fellowship with mankind, and so He created him a free moral agent. God could have made a bunch of robots. God could have made mechanical men and pushed a button to make them bow down to Him. But God didn't want that kind of a man. God wanted a man to be free to choose Him and to love Him and to serve Him.

My friend, in the midst of all the unbelief, the blasphemy, and the hostility toward God which is around us today, the greatest thing you can do as a human being is to publicly choose the Lord Jesus Christ. To believe in God the Father Almighty, the Maker of heaven and earth and to receive His Son, Jesus Christ, is the most glorious privilege that you and I have. We hear a lot of talk about freedom of speech and freedom of every sort, but this poor crowd around us who talks so loudly of freedom doesn't seem to know what freedom really is. We have real freedom when we choose Jesus Christ as our Savior.

Now let's return to the first verse of Genesis: "In the beginning God created the heaven and the earth." This is a majestic verse. It is a tremendous verse. I am of the opinion that it is the doorway through which you will have to walk into the Bible. You have to believe that God is the Creator, for he that cometh to God must believe that He *is.* "In the beginning God created the heaven and the earth."

"In the beginning"—that is a beginning which you cannot date. You can estimate it as billions of years, and I think you would be accurate, but who knows how many? Certainly *man* does not know.

"God created." The word "create" is from the Hebrew word *bara,* which means to create out of nothing. This word is used only three times in the first chapter of Genesis, because it records only three acts of creation. (1) The creation of something from nothing: "In the beginning God created the heaven and the earth." (2) The creation of life: "And God created great whales, and every living creature that moveth . . ." (v. 21). That's animal life of all kinds. (3) The creation of man: "So God created man in his own image . . ." (v. 27). Theistic evolution is not the answer. It attempts to follow creation until the time of man, then considers Adam and Eve to be products of some evolutionary process. The theistic evolutionist considers the days in Genesis as periods of time, long periods of time. I do not believe that is true. God's marking off the creative days with the words, "And the evening and the morning were the first day," etc., makes it clear that He was not referring to long periods of time but to actual twenty-four hour days.

"God created the heaven and the earth." The earth is separated from the rest of creation. Why? Well, the earth is the hometown of mankind; that's where he is to be placed. We are very much interested in him because we belong to this creature. We need to realize, my friend, that you and I are creatures, creatures of God, and as creatures of God, we owe Him something.

It was years ago that Herbert Spencer said, "The most general forms into which the manifestation of the Unknowable are re-divisible are *time, space, matter, force, motion.*" Those were his categories of division. A very fine personal worker, George Dewey Blomgren, was talking to an army sergeant who was a law graduate. Mr. Blomgren was attempting to witness to him. The sergeant mentioned Herbert Spencer, so Mr. Blomgren replied, "Did you know that both the Bible and Spencer teach the great principle of creation?" The sergeant's eyes widened and he asked, "How's that?" The reply was, "Spencer talked about time, space, matter, force, motion. In the first two verses of Genesis we find: 'In the beginning [time] God created the heaven [space] and the earth [matter]. And the earth was without form and void; and darkness was upon the face of the deep. And the Spirit of God [force] moved [motion] upon the face of the waters.' It took Spencer fifty years to uncover this law, but here it is in fifty seconds." The sergeant had no grounds for argument and soon trusted Christ as his Savior.

It is very interesting that God has put down these great principles in the first two verses of Genesis. How important it is for us to see that.

And the earth was without form, and void; and darkness was upon the face of the deep. And the spirit of God moved upon the face of the waters [Gen. 1:2].

Although this view has been discredited by many in the past few years, I believe that a great catastrophe took place between verses 1 and 2. As far as I can see, there is an abundance of evidence for it. To begin with, look out upon this vast creation—something has happened to it! Man's trip to the moon reveals nothing in the world but a wasteland up there. How did it get that way? May I say that there came a catastrophe in God's universe.

That is specifically mentioned in regard to the earth because this is to be the place where man lives, and so the earth is described as being "without form and void."

"Darkness was upon the face of the deep" indicates the absence of God, of course.

"Without form, and void" is a very interesting expression. "Without form" is the Hebrew word *tohu*, meaning a ruin, vacancy; "void" is the Hebrew word *bohu*, meaning emptiness. Notice this statement in the prophecy of Isaiah: "For thus said the LORD that created the heavens; God himself that formed the earth and made it; he hath established it, he created it not in vain, he formed it to be inhabited: I am the LORD; and there is none else" (Isa. 45:18). Here God says that He did not create the earth "in vain," and the Hebrew word is *tohu*, which is the same word we found in Genesis 1:2. God did not create the earth without form and void. God created this universe a cosmos, not a chaos. This is the thing which Isaiah is attempting to make clear. He created it not *tohu va bohu*, but the earth became *tohu va bohu*. God formed the earth to be inhabited, and it was God who came to this wreck and made it a habitable place for mankind.

Our current study and exploration of space has revealed, so far, that you and I live in a universe in which only the earth is habitable for human beings. I believe that Genesis is telling us that this earth *became* without form and void, that it was just as uninhabitable as the moon when the Spirit of God moved upon the face of the waters.

I believe that the entire universe came under this great catastrophe. What was the catastrophe? We can only suggest that there was some pre-Adamic creature that was on this earth. And it seems that all of this is connected with the fall of Lucifer, son of the morning, who became Satan, the Devil, as we know him today. I think all of this is involved here, but God has not given us details. The fact of the matter is that He has given us very, very few details in the first chapter of Genesis.

"And the spirit of God moved." The word for "moved" means brooded, like a mother hen broods over her little chicks. He brooded upon the face of the waters. The Holy Spirit began a ministry here which we will find Him doing again and again. It is re-creation! He comes into this scene and He recreates. This is precisely what He does for us.

You will remember that the Lord Jesus said, ". . . Except a man be born of water and of the Spirit, he cannot enter into the kingdom of God" (John 3:5). The water is the Word of God. Now, if you want to make baptism the symbol for it, that's fine. But the water means the Word of God. And the Holy Spirit is the Author of it. This is very important for us to see.

CONSTRUCTION OF THE EARTH

We have seen the construction of the universe in verse 1, the convulsion of the earth in verse 2, and now we come to the construction of the earth in six days (vv. 3–31). I believe what we have here is this development.

There are several things here that I would like to call to your attention. In Exodus 20:11, it reads "For in six days the LORD made heaven and earth, the sea, and all that in them is. . . ." There is nothing in that verse about creating. It says "made"; God is taking that which is already formed and in these six days He is not "creating" but He is re-creating. He is working with matter which already exists, out of the matter which He had called into existence probably billions of years before.

God created life and put it on the earth, and for the earth He created man. That is the creature we are interested in because you and I happen to be one of those creatures. This makes the Genesis record intensely important for us today.

DAY ONE—LIGHT

And God said, Let there be light: and there was light.

And God saw the light, that it was good: and God divided the light from the darkness.

And God called the light Day, and the darkness he called Night. And the evening and the morning were the first day [Gen. 1:3–5].

That must have been a twenty-four hour day—I don't see how you could get anything else out of it. Notice that God said, "Let there be light." Ten times in this chapter we will find "let there be"—let there be a firmament, let there be lights, let the waters be gathered together, etc. Someone has called these the ten commandments of creation. This is the divine decalogue that we find here.

"God said, Let there be light." This is the first time we are told that God spoke. These are His first words recorded in Scripture.

DAY TWO—AIR SPACES

And God said, Let there be a firmament in the midst of the waters, and let it divide the waters from the waters [Gen. 1:6].

"God said, Let there be a firmament"—the Hebrew word for firmament is *raqia*, meaning air spaces.

"Let it divide the waters from the waters." What does that mean?

Well, God first divided the waters perpendicularly. There is water above us and water beneath us.

And God made the firmament, and divided the waters which were under the firmament from the waters which were above the firmament: and it was so [Gen. 1:7].

Out in the Hawaiian Islands, when we were there one year, five inches of rain fell in Honolulu in just a very short time—I started to say in a few minutes and I think I'm accurate in that. We were in a place where over two hundred inches of rain fall in a year. My friend, there is a whole lot of water up there if two hundred inches of it can fall! Well, that's what God did. He divided the waters above from the waters which are beneath.

And God called the firmament Heaven. And the evening and the morning were the second day [Gen. 1:8].

"God called the firmament Heaven." This is not heaven as you and I think of it. Actually, there are three heavens that are mentioned in Scripture. The Lord Jesus spoke of the birds of heaven, and I think that is the heaven mentioned in this verse. Then there are the stars of heaven, meaning the second heaven, and there is the third heaven where God dwells. So the first layer up there, the first deck, is the deck where the clouds are and where the birds fly.

DAY THREE—DRY LAND AND PLANT LIFE

And God said, Let the waters under the heaven be gathered together unto one place, and let the dry land appear: and it was so.

And God called the dry land Earth; and the gathering together of the waters called he Seas: and God saw that it was good [Gen. 1:9–10].

Now there is a horizontal division made of the waters. First the waters above were separated from the waters beneath. Now the water is separated from the land, from the earth. May I say to you, there is nothing unscientific about this. They tell us that every spot on topside of this earth on which we live today was covered with water at one time. That was evidently a judgment that had come upon the earth way back sometime in the distant eternity of the past, and we know practically nothing about it. Anything we say is speculation. God has really told us very little here. But He has told us enough so that we can believe Him, that's all.

"God called the dry land Earth." What is He getting ready to do? Well, it looks like He is getting ready to make a place where He can put man, a place that is habitable. Man is not a water creature, even though there are evolutionists who think we came from the sea and from seaweed, as we mentioned, and others who think we came out of a slop bucket! How absurd can they possibly be?

And God said, Let the earth bring forth grass, the herb yielding seed, and the fruit tree yielding fruit after his kind, whose seed is in itself, upon the earth: and it was so [Gen. 1:11].

Now God is putting plant life here because man, until the Flood, was a vegetarian. Man will eat nothing but fruit and nuts. The forming of the plant life completed the third day.

And the earth brought forth grass, and herb yielding seed after his kind, and the tree yielding fruit, whose seed was in itself, after his kind: and God saw that it was good.

And the evening and the morning were the third day [Gen. 1:12–13].

DAY FOUR—SUN, MOON, STARS APPEAR

And God said, Let there be lights in the firmament of the heaven to divide the day from the night; and let them be for signs, and for seasons, and for days, and years [Gen. 1:14].

God didn't create the sun and the moon at this time. They were already up there. God just brought them around into position.

And let them be for lights in the firmament of the heaven to give light upon the earth: and it was so.

And God made two great lights; the greater light to rule the day, and the lesser light to rule the night: he made the stars also [Gen. 1:15–16].

One of them was to take charge of the day, and the sun does that pretty well. Also the moon does a good job by night. I don't know about you, but I proposed to my wife by moonlight. That moon has a lot of influence over the night, I can assure you.

Then there is just a little clause, "He made the stars also." That was a pretty big job, by the way, but not for God. It was John Wesley who said, "God created the heavens and the earth and didn't even half try." God "made the stars also."

And God set them in the firmament of the heaven to give light upon the earth,

And to rule over the day and over the night, and to divide the light from the darkness: and God saw that it was good [Gen. 1:17–18].

You will notice that it is God who does the dividing here, "to divide the light from the darkness."

You know, He still does that! There are those today who ask,

"What's the difference between right and wrong?" God has drawn all the lines. How can we know what is right? God says what is right. God has put down certain principles. God divides the light from the darkness and there is just that much distinction between right and wrong. He is the One who makes the difference, and He still does it.

And the evening and the morning were the fourth day [Gen. 1:19].

DAY FIVE—ANIMAL LIFE

And God said, Let the waters bring forth abundantly the moving creature that hath life, and fowl that may fly above the earth in the open firmament of heaven [Gen. 1:20].

We do have a certain amount of development. This does not mean that everything came from one little cell but that God made one of each creature and there has been development from each one. God said, "Let the waters bring forth abundantly," and the next verse adds "after their kind." The word "kind" does not mean species, as even Darwin said, but it means more than that. The word is phylum. I have been reading that one scientist said he had been looking around for another word. Well, I had a professor in seminary, a very brilliant man, who gave phylum as a synonym for "kind." If you will look up that word in the dictionary, you will see that it means a direct line of descent within a group. For instance, it would include not just one horse but every animal in the horse family. God created one like that, and there has been development from each one, tremendous development. Also there has been devolution—that is, there has been development, then later there has been degeneration.

And God created great whales, and every living creature that moveth, which the waters brought forth abundantly, after their kind, and every winged fowl after his kind: and God saw that it was good [Gen. 1:21].

"And God saw that it was good." Notice that. When God does it, it's *good*.

> **And God blessed them, saying, Be fruitful, and multiply, and fill the waters in the seas, and let fowl multiply in the earth [Gen. 1:22].**

By the way, one scientist I quoted previously said that if our schools teach the creation story, they might as well teach the stork story. Believe me, the Bible certainly gets rid of the stork story. If you read it carefully, you will notice that these animals had to "bring forth." This will be true of mankind also. You won't find little Willie under a stump, and the stork won't bring little Susie, either.

> **And the evening and the morning were the fifth day [Gen. 1:23].**

DAY SIX—FERTILITY OF ANIMAL LIFE

> **And God said, Let the earth bring forth the living creature after his kind, cattle, and creeping thing, and beast of the earth after his kind: and it was so.**
>
> **And God made the beast of the earth after his kind, and cattle after their kind, and every thing that creepeth upon the earth after his kind: and God saw that it was good [Gen. 1:24–25].**

Notice again the expression "after his kind"—after his biological phylum. Now we will see that God separates plant life and animal life from mankind, and He says, "Let us make man in our image." This creature is of great interest to you because he happens to be your great-great, etc., grandfather, and he is mine, also. This means that you and I are cousins, although maybe not kissing cousins. But the whole human family is related.

CREATION OF MAN

And God said, Let us make man in our image, after our likeness: and let them have dominion over the fish of the sea, and over the fowl of the air, and over the cattle, and over all the earth, and over every creeping thing that creepeth upon the earth [Gen. 1:26].

The first question that arises is: *How* was man created? The next chapter will tell us that. "And let them have dominion." God gave him dominion over the earth, and I do not think this means that God made him a sort of glorified gardener of the Garden of Eden. Adam had tremendous authority given to him. We will find out a little later that God says to him that he is to do certain things relative to this creation that God has given to him.

So God created man in his own image, in the image of God created he him; male and female created he them [Gen. 1:27].

We have here just the simple fact of the creation of man. This is the third time we find the word *bara*, which means to create out of nothing. So we see that man is created; he is something new. *Bara* is the same word that occurred in the first verse of Genesis: "In the beginning God *created* the heaven and the earth." He created the physical universe. Then He created life: "And God *created* great whales, and every living creature that moveth . . ." (1:21). Now we see that God created man: "So God *created* man in his own image." God will give us the details of His creation of man in the next chapter, and we can see from this that God has left out a great deal about the creation of the universe. "In the beginning God created the heaven and the earth" is all the information He has given to us, and it's about all we can know about it. He could have filled in details, but He didn't. He will go into more detail about only one act of His creation, and that is His creation of man. Do you know why? It is because this record was written for

man; God wants him to know about his origin. It is as if God were
saying, "I would like very much for you to pay attention to your own
creation and not be speculating about the creation of the universe."
This verse tells us something tremendous.

"So God created man in his own image." I want to submit to you
that this is one of the great statements of the Word of God. I cannot
conceive of anything quite as wonderful as this. What does it mean?
Well, man is like God, I think, as a trinity. Immediately someone is
going to say, "Oh, I know what you mean. You mean that man is physically and mentally and spiritually a being." Yes, I believe that is true.
Paul, in 1 Thessalonians 5:23, says that very thing: ". . . And I pray
God your whole spirit and soul and body be preserved blameless unto
the coming of our Lord Jesus Christ." Although this is true, we will
see when we get into the next chapter that it actually means more than
that. I think that it refers to the fact that man is a personality, and as a
personality he is self-conscious, and he is one who makes his own
decisions. He is a free moral agent. Apparently that is the thing which
is unique about mankind. I believe this is what is meant by God creating man in His own image.

"Male and female created he them." These verses do not give to us
the details of how man was created and how woman was created. We
won't find that until we come to the second chapter. That is the reason
that I say that God did not intend to give us the details concerning the
creation of this great universe that we are in or He would have given
us another chapter relative to that. But He offers no explanation other
than He is the Creator. This puts us right back to the all-important
truth which we find in the eleventh chapter of Hebrews: "Through
faith we understand that the worlds were framed by the word of God,
so that things which are seen were not made of things which do appear" (Heb. 11:3). Things we see today were made out of things which
did not even exist before. The creation was made ex nihilo, out of
nothing. Somebody says, "Explain that." My friend, I can't explain it.
And evolution doesn't explain it either. Evolution has never answered
the question of how nothing becomes something. It always starts with
a little amoeba, or with a garbage can, or with a little piece of sea-

weed, or with an animal up in a tree. Our minds must have something to start with, but the Bible starts with nothing. God created! This is the tremendous revelation of this chapter.

And God blessed them, and God said unto them, Be fruitful, and multiply, and replenish the earth, and subdue it: and have dominion over the fish of the sea, and over the fowl of the air, and over every living thing that moveth upon the earth [Gen. 1:28].

We see here that God has given to this creature something unusual. First He says to man, "Be fruitful, and multiply, and replenish the earth." We will hear Him repeat that when He creates woman. God seems to be the One who introduced the subject of sex. It is quite interesting that our generation thinks that they have made a new discovery, that they are the Columbus that discovered sex. God mentions it here at the very beginning. In fact, there are four methods that God has used to get mankind into this universe. One was by *direct* creation, which produced Adam. A second way was by *indirect* creation, which produced Eve. The third was by the *virgin birth,* and this was how Jesus Christ came into the human family. The fourth way is by *natural generation,* and that is pretty well known in our day.

We have certainly dragged natural generation down to a level that God never intended for it. God created man to reproduce. This is a wonderful, glorious truth, and it is not to be made into a dirty, filthy, slimy thing as man is doing now. People are writing dirty, filthy books and calling it literature; they are producing dirty, filthy things and calling it art. Some of the critics are beginning to speak out against this, and we thank the Lord for that. They are saying what I have long contended, that much of what is called art is revolting and repulsive and that it is not art at all. It is nothing in the world but obscene, and it is done simply for the almighty *dollar.* God never intended for sex to be abused in this way.

God created this man in His image. God is the essentially personal Being, and in giving the man an immortal soul, He gave him also a true personality. Man has a self-consciousness, he has the power of free choice, and he has a distinct moral responsibility. He is in the image of God.

"Be fruitful, and multiply, and replenish the earth." God tells man to fill the earth by reproduction. And notice that He uses the word "replenish." That is an interesting word and seems to indicate that this earth had been inhabited before by other creatures. Whatever the creatures were, they had disappeared before man was created.

God also tells man to "subdue" the earth. This, I think, is the basis of learning and of scientific exploration in our day. One of the Proverbs says this: "It is the glory of God to conceal a thing: but the honour of kings is to search out a matter" (Prov. 25:2).

God hides diamonds way down in the earth and God also puts the treasures down where man has to dig for them, and I believe that today the same thing is true about knowledge. I think it is true about the study of the Word of God. God wants us to go into the laboratory to use the test tube and the microscope, but unfortunately man comes out with an atom bomb, and he is trying to destroy the human family in our day.

"And have dominion" is God's instruction to man. Adam was not just a gardener to cut the grass. Man was created to rule this earth. I think that Adam could control the weather just as we control the air-conditioning in our homes. He *ruled* this earth. This is what we see in the Lord Jesus. When He was here on this earth, He had control over nature. He could say to a storm, "Be still." He could feed a multitude with five loaves and two fishes. It is my opinion that Adam could have done all of that until his fall. At the Fall he lost the dominion that God had given him.

And God said, Behold, I have given you every herb bearing seed, which is upon the face of all the earth, and every tree, in which is the fruit of a tree yielding seed; to you it shall be for meat [Gen. 1:29].

From this statement I assume that man was a vegetarian at first, and not until after the Flood did man become a meat eater.

And to every beast of the earth, and to every fowl of the air, and to every thing that creepeth upon the earth, wherein there is life, I have given every green herb for meat: and it was so.

And God saw everything that he had made, and, behold, it was very good. And the evening and the morning were the sixth day [Gen. 1:30–31].

This brings us to the end of chapter one, and it might be well to make a resumé at this point. What are some of the things we should note here? Well, one of these things is the fact that God is mentioned here thirty-two times. The Bible makes no attempt to prove that there is a God. Why not? Because He says, "The fool hath said in his heart, There is no God . . ." (Ps. 14:1).

The Bible is a Book written to reveal the spiritual, the religious, the redemptive truth, and that comes to us only by *faith*. So we have here the fact that God is the One who created.

In this first chapter we see the unity and power and personality of God. This is exactly what Paul wrote in Romans 1:20: "For the invisible things of him from the creation of the world are clearly seen." How are they clearly seen? "Being understood by the things that are made, even his eternal power and Godhead; so that they are without excuse." I say to you very candidly that God has shut you up to *faith* in Himself.

We will notice some other truths in this chapter. It denies polytheism: *One* God creates. Secondly, it denies the eternity of matter. The first words are: "In the beginning"—and it all had a beginning, my friend. This is true in spite of the fact that there was a time when science taught the eternity of matter. Thirdly, this chapter denies pantheism. God is before all things and He is apart from them. Fourthly, it denies fatalism—God acts in the freedom of His will.

Finally, let me enumerate the striking features in chapter 1:

(1) Order
(2) Progress
(3) Promptness
(4) Perfection

CHAPTER 2

THEME: The Sabbath Day; summary of the first five
days of the restoration; man's creation; condition
placed on man; woman's creation

A great principle of revelation occurs for the first time in this chapter, but it will be found again and again in the Word of God. It is
one of the fingerprints of inspiration. It is the law of recurrence or the
law of recapitulation. In other words, the Spirit of God, in giving the
Word of God, has a practice of stating briefly a series of great facts and
truths; then He will come back and take out of the series that which is
all-important, and He will elucidate and enlarge upon that particular
thing. He is going to do this now in chapter 2 with the six days of
creation which were given in chapter 1. This same principle is seen in
the Book of Deuteronomy. Deuteronomy is the interpretation of the
Law after forty years of experience with it in the wilderness. Deuteronomy is not just a repetition of the Law, but rather an interpretation
of it. Likewise, we are given not only one but *four* Gospels. Again and
again, this procedure is followed throughout the Word of God.

THE SABBATH DAY

In chapter 2 that which is lifted out of the six days of creation is that
which pertains to man, and we begin with the Sabbath Day.

**Thus the heavens and the earth were finished, and all
the host of them.**

**And on the seventh day God ended his work which he
had made; and he rested on the seventh day from all his
work which he had made.**

**And God blessed the seventh day, and sanctified it: be-
cause that in it he had rested from all his work which
God created and made [Gen. 2:1–3].**

Do not miss the importance of the Sabbath Day. What does it mean when it says that God rested from His work? Does it mean that God got tired, sat down to rest on the seventh day, and said that he had had a big week—that He had worked more than forty hours, and that He wanted to rest? If you look at it like that, it is perfect nonsense. God rested *from* His work. When God finished His six days of work, He looked upon it and it was very good, and there was nothing else to do. Every time I leave my office for the day, I still have work all over my desk. I have never been able to sit down and say, "I'm through. I've finished it." But *God* did. At the end of six days, He rested the seventh day because His work was complete. This is one of the greatest spiritual truths there is. The Book of Hebrews tells us that as believers we enter into "rest"—that is, we enter into His *sabbath;* we enter into His perfect redemption. He died on the cross almost two thousand years ago for you and me, and He offers us a redemption that we can enter into. Thus Paul can write: "Therefore being justified by faith, we have peace with God through our Lord Jesus Christ" (Rom. 5:1). I do not even have to lift my little finger in order to be saved—Jesus did it all.

> Jesus paid it all,
> All to Him I owe;
> Sin had left a crimson stain,
> He washed it white as snow.
> —Mrs. H. M. Hall

SUMMARY OF THE FIRST FIVE DAYS
OF RESTORATION

Apparently, this vast universe we live in had been here for billions of years, but something happened to the earth and to a great deal of the creation. As a result, God moved in, the Spirit of God moved upon the face of the deep, and there was brought cosmos out of chaos.

These are the generations of the heavens and of the earth when they were created, in the day that the LORD God made the earth and the heavens [Gen. 2:4].

Actually, the word "generations" means *families*. The Book of Genesis is not only the book of beginnings but also the book of the families. "These are the families of the heavens and of the earth when they were created, in the day that the LORD God made the earth and the heavens."

And every plant of the field before it was in the earth, and every herb of the field before it grew: for the LORD God had not caused it to rain upon the earth, and there was not a man to till the ground.

But there went up a mist from the earth, and watered the whole face of the ground [Gen. 2:5–6].

All this was here long before man was here upon the earth, and we can now begin to discover the purpose of God in chapter 1. In chapter 1 God was preparing a home for the man whom He would make. God is now getting ready to move this man into a place that He has prepared for him.

MAN'S CREATION

In the first chapter we saw that there was nothing, and then the inorganic came into existence: "In the beginning God created the heaven and the earth." The next step in creation was the organic, that is, the creation of life. We saw that in verse 21 where it says that God created great whales and then all animal life. He created animal life, but apparently the plant life had not been destroyed, and at the time of the re-creation, the seed was already in the earth. I would not want to be dogmatic, but this would seem to be the implication here. God has told us very little in this regard. Then man is the next step in the creation. There is actually no natural transition, and evolution cannot bridge the gap that brings us to the appearance of Homo sapiens on the earth. The earth, therefore, was prepared for the coming of man.

And the LORD God formed man of the dust of the ground, and breathed into his nostrils the breath of life; and man became a living soul [Gen. 2:7].

This is the method of the creation of man, and again we are limited in what God has told us. Physically, man was taken out of the ground. It is quite interesting that our bodies are made up of about fifteen or sixteen chemical elements. Those same chemical elements are in the ground. The physical part of man was taken out of the dust of the ground. If we were to be boiled down into the separate chemical elements of which we are made, we would be worth very little in terms of money. I used to say $2.98, but inflation has increased that figure a little. That is the extent of our bodily worth because we were made out of the dust of the ground.

But man is more than dust. Physically, dust he is and to the dust he will return, but his spirit is going to God. Why? Because God "breathed into his nostrils the breath of life; and man became a living soul." God breathed into him "the breath of life." God gave man life which is physical or psychological, and then He gave him life which is spiritual. In other words, man now is brought into a marvelous relationship with his Creator. He has in his being a capacity for God. This is what separates man from all other creatures that are found in God's universe, as far as we know. Of course, there are the angels, but we know very little about them.

The theistic evolutionists say that mankind evolved up to this point, and then God began to work with this product of evolution. However, no form of evolutionary theory can account for human speech, it cannot account for human conscience, and it cannot account for human individuality. These are three things with which evolution has a little difficulty. It is mighty easy to take the bones of a man and compare them to the bones of some anthropoid, probably an ape, or to a horse. There is a striking similarity, I am sure, and yet there is a wide divergence also. I would expect that there would be a certain similarity because these creatures are to move in the same environment in which we move as human beings—naturally, the chassis would have to be the same. For example, there is a very striking similarity between the chassis of a Ford automobile and that of a Chevrolet automobile, but you had better not say that to the Ford Motor Company or to General Motors! They will tell you that there is a *wide* difference between the two. But there is a very striking similarity when you see the chassis. You must begin with something fixed on which you can put four wheels, one on each corner, and it must be rectangular to a certain extent. Why? Because the Ford and the Chevrolet are both going to get stuck on the freeway at five o'clock in the afternoon. A car must be able to balance, and it must have a motor to move it. So you would have a similarity, but that does not mean they came out of the same factory. I feel that such an exaggeration has been made of the similarity between man and these other creatures. Man is a different creature. God breathed into his breathing places the breath of life, and man became a living soul. Man is fearfully and wonderfully made, and that is something which we need to keep in mind.

> **And the LORD God planted a garden eastward in Eden; and there he put the man whom he had formed [Gen. 2:8].**

I cannot tell you where the Garden of Eden is. I am sure it is somewhere in the Tigris-Euphrates Valley; in fact it may be the entire valley. Originally, that valley was a very fertile place, and it still is, for that matter. It is part of "the fertile crescent." At one time, the peoples inhabiting that region did not even plant grain there; they simply harvested it, for it grew by itself. It is probable that this area will someday become the very center of the earth again.

> **And out of the ground made the LORD God to grow every tree that is pleasant to the sight, and good for food; the tree of life also in the midst of the garden, and the tree of knowledge of good and evil [Gen. 2:9].**

These are unusual trees that are mentioned specifically, the "tree of life" and the "tree of knowledge of good and evil." I cannot tell you much about them because they are not around today; they have been removed from the scene.

The Lord God made "to grow every tree," and the trees, you will notice, were pleasant to look at and were also good for food. There was the beauty of them and the practical side of them; both were combined in them. Perhaps it can be compared to going into a furniture store and having the salesman say, "This article of furniture is very beautiful, but it's also very functional." That was the important thing in the Garden of Eden—they had some beautiful trees, but they were also functional. In fact, they were very practical—they were good for food. On this earth on which we live, we still see something of its beauty. In spite of the curse of the fall of man which is upon the earth—the fact that it brings forth the thorn and the thistle—there is still a beauty here. I remember the first time I visited the place called Hana on the island of Maui in the Hawaiian Islands. It is difficult to get there, but as we drove down that road, I had never been in such fabulous, fantastic, and wonderful foliage in my life. It is beyond description. We made a certain turn and came upon a very scenic spot. We could look down that coast and see a little peninsula protruding. There were the coconut trees, the papaya trees, the hibiscus, the bananas, the bamboo; and among the coconut trees a little church stood which the missionaries had started. We just could not help but be startled by its beauty. In fact, so much so that as we stood there, I asked the tour group with me to pause and bow their heads in prayer, and a member of our party led us in prayer. We were just privileged to see that spot. My, the Garden of Eden must have been a beautiful place!

> **And a river went out of Eden to water the garden; and from thence it was parted, and became into four heads.**
>
> **The name of the first is Pison: that is it which compasseth the whole land of Havilah, where there is gold:**
>
> **And the gold of that land is good: there is bdellium and the onyx stone.**
>
> **And the name of the second river is Gihon: the same is it that compasseth the whole land of Ethiopia.**
>
> **And the name of the third river is Hiddekel: that is it which goeth toward the east of Assyria. And the fourth river is Euphrates [Gen. 2:10–14].**

The river in Ethiopia would be the Nile, and the Hiddekel would be the Tigris.

And the LORD God took the man, and put him into the garden of Eden to dress it and to keep it [Gen. 2:15].

This man had dominion, and the forces of nature responded at his beck and call.

CONDITION PLACED ON MAN

And the LORD God commanded the man, saying, Of every tree of the garden thou mayest freely eat:

But of the tree of the knowledge of good and evil, thou shalt not eat of it: for in the day that thou eatest thereof thou shalt surely die [Gen. 2:16–17].

It was not God's original intention for man to die, but man is now put on probation. You see, man has a free will, and privilege always creates responsibility. This is an axiomatic statement that is true. This man who is given a free will must be given a test to determine whether he will obey God or not.

Some expositors suggest that the fruit of the tree of the knowledge of good and evil was poison. On the contrary, I think it was the best fruit in the garden.

"For in the day that thou eatest thereof thou shalt surely die." Remember that man is a trinity, and he would have to die in a threefold way. Adam did not die physically until over nine hundred years after this, but God said, "In the day you eat, you shall die." Death means separation, and Adam was separated from God spiritually the very day he ate, you may be sure of that.

And the LORD God said, It is not good that the man should be alone; I will make him an help meet for him [Gen. 2:18].

There is a purpose in God's putting man in the garden alone for a period of time. It was to show him that he had a need, that he needed someone to be with him.

> **And out of the ground the LORD God formed every beast of the field, and every fowl of the air; and brought them unto Adam to see what he would call them: and whatsoever Adam called every living creature, that was the name thereof [Gen. 2:19].**

Believe me, that man had to be a smart man to name all the animals. Some wag has said that when God brought an elephant to Adam and said, "What shall we call this one?" Adam said, "Well, he looks more like an elephant than anything else." And I guess he did!

> **And Adam gave names to all cattle, and to the fowl of the air, and to every beast of the field; but for Adam there was not found an help meet for him [Gen. 2:20].**

"An help for him"—(the word *meet* should not be here)—that is, one agreeing and answering to him, a helper as his counterpart, the other half of him. A man is but half a man until he is married, and that is very important to see. I am not here to promote marriage, and yet I would say that it is God's intention for both man and woman. The woman is to answer to the man.

WOMAN'S CREATION

> **And the LORD God caused a deep sleep to fall upon Adam, and he slept: and he took one of his ribs, and closed up the flesh instead thereof;**

> **And the rib, which the LORD God had taken from man, made he a woman, and brought her unto the man [Gen. 2:21–22].**

The woman is taken from Adam, from the side of Adam. Dr. Matthew Henry said that God didn't take her from the head to be his superior, or from his foot to be his inferior, but He took her from his side to be equal with him, to be along with him. That is exactly the purpose: she is to be the other half of man. This is exactly what God meant when He said, "Wives, submit to your husbands." He means that she is to respond, to answer to him. A wife is the other part of him, the other half of him. He is only half a man without her.

Believe me, Eve was beautiful. Any woman today who is beautiful inherited it originally from mother Eve. There is no beauty that she did not have. She was a doll, let me tell you! And she was the other half of Adam.

And Adam said, This is now bone of my bones, and flesh of my flesh: she shall be called Woman, because she was taken out of Man [Gen. 2:23].

The word for "Woman" in the Hebrew language is very similar to the word for "Man." The word for man is ish, and the word for woman is ishshah. She is the other part of man and is to answer to him. God intended man to take the lead—He created him first—and He created woman to follow. The man is the aggressor—God made him that way even physically—and woman is the responder.

Do not tell me that a wife has to love her husband. God does not say that. God says that she is to respond to him. If he says to her, "I love you," then she is going to say right back to him, "I love you." When a man tells me, "My wife is very cold," that is a dead giveaway that he is not really the kind of husband he should be. If he is the right kind of husband, she will respond, because he is the one to take the lead.

Therefore shall man leave his father and his mother, and shall cleave unto his wife: and they shall be one flesh [Gen. 2:24].

In other words, the man is now subject to his wife in the sense that he is responsible for her, and he is no longer under the control of his father and mother.

And they were both naked, the man and his wife, and were not ashamed [Gen. 2:25].

Although the Scriptures do not say so, I believe they were clothed with some sort of glory light. May I say, I think that this is the loveliest and the most precious account of the creation of woman and man. Here is a couple whom God really joined together. There are certain things which God has given to His people that they should obey, and God has given to the human race marriage. Marriage is one of the bands which modern men are trying to throw off: "Let us break their bands asunder, and cast away their cords from us" (Ps. 2:3). What is man trying to do? He is trying to get rid of God, because God is the One who established marriage.

The creation of woman was indirect creation, for God took her out of man to reveal the fact that she is part of man. Someone has put it like this: "For woman is not undeveloped man, but diverse, not like to like, but like in difference. Yet in the long years, 'liker' must they grow, till at the last she set herself to man like perfect music unto noble words, distinct in individualities, but like each other even as those who love." The story of creation of woman for man is one of the most beautiful stories.

The subjects of this chapter are quite wonderful: the creation of man, where he is placed, his occupation, the condition upon which he is there with a responsibility, his need for a companion, and then God's creation of woman. There is to be an identity between the husband and the wife, and God says, "Husbands, love your wives." This is the creation story.

The man who was the chaplain at Nuremberg Prison and dealt with men who had been Nazi chiefs has written of his experiences. Speaking of his last interview with Herman Goering, one of the very few who refused to accept Christ, Chaplain Gerecke says, "That evening, around 8:30 I had a long session with Goering—during which he made sport of the story of creation, ridiculed divine inspiration of the Scriptures and made outright denial of certain Christian fundamentals." *Less than two hours later he committed suicide.* My friend, one of the ways to get rid of the alarming suicide rate is to let men and women know they are creatures of God who are responsible to their Creator. How important this is!

We have seen in chapter 2 man's kinship with God, man's worship of God, man's fellowship with God, man's service to God, man's loyalty to God, man's authority from God, and man's social life from and for God. This is the great message of this chapter.

CHAPTER 3

THEME: The serpent denies the Word of God; the man and woman disobey the Word of God; the design of God for the future; the doctrine of redemption introduced

We come now to what some consider to be the most important chapter of the Bible. It is conceded, I believe, by all conservative expositors to be just that. Dr. Griffith Thomas called chapter 3 the pivot of the Bible. If you doubt that, read chapters 1 and 2 of Genesis, omit chapter 3, and then read chapters 4—11. You will find that there is a tremendous vacuum that needs to be filled, that something has happened. For instance, in Genesis 1 and 2, we find man in innocence; everything is perfection, and there is fellowship between God and man. But the minute you begin with chapter 4 of Genesis and read just as far as chapter 11, you find jealousy, anger, murder, lying, wickedness, corruption, rebellion, and judgment. The question is: Where did it all come from? Where did it begin? Where did the sin originate? Actually, I do not think it originated in chapter 3 of Genesis, but as far as man is concerned, here is where it began.

Let me quote for you the statement of another concerning chapter 3:

"Here we trace back to their source many of the rivers of divine truth. Here commences the great drama which is being enacted on the stage of human history and which well nigh 6,000 years has not yet completed. Here we find the divine explanation of the present fallen and ruined condition of our race. Here we learn of the subtle devices of our enemy, the devil. Here we behold the utter powerlessness of man to walk in the path of righteousness when divine grace is withheld from him. Here we discover the spiritual effects of sin, man seeking to flee from God. Here we discern the attitude of God toward the guilty sinner. Here we mark the universal tendency of human nature to cover its own moral shame by a device of man's own handiwork. Here we are taught of the gracious provision which God has made to meet our great need. Here begins that marvelous stream of prophecy which runs all through the Holy Scriptures. Here we learn that man cannot approach God except through a mediator."

THE SERPENT CASTS A SHADOW
OF DOUBT ON THE WORD OF GOD

In this first section we have the setting for the temptation of man.

Now the serpent was more subtil than any beast of the field which the LORD God had made. And he said unto the woman, Yea, hath God said, Ye shall not eat of every tree of the garden? [Gen. 3:1].

The question arises: Why the temptation? If we go back to chapters 1 and 2, we find that man was created innocent, but man was not created righteous. What is righteousness? Righteousness is innocence that has been maintained in the presence of temptation. You see, temptation will either develop you or destroy you; it will do one of the two. The Garden of Eden was not a hothouse, and man was not a hothouse plant. Character must be developed, and it can only be developed in the presence of temptation. Man was created a responsible being, and he was responsible to glorify, to obey, to serve, and to be subject to divine government.

Man did not create himself—I do not think anyone claims that—but God created him. And God was not arbitrary in the condition which He laid down. He said to man, "But of the tree of the knowledge of good and evil, thou shalt not eat of it: for in the day that thou eatest thereof thou shalt surely die" (Gen. 2:17). That tree was not the only tree in the garden to eat of. It would have been very arbitrary if man would have starved to death if he had not been able to eat of the tree and if he had also been told he would die if he did eat of it. There was an abundance of trees in the garden which bore fruit; so that man did not need to eat of this tree at all. Therefore, we find that man appears on the scene a responsible creature.

In this first verse we are introduced to the serpent. Immediately the question can reasonably be asked, "Where in the world did he come from? How did he get into the Garden of Eden?" As far as I can tell from the Word of God, the serpent was not there as a slithering creature. Actually, we are not told how he came there; we are just told he was there. The Word of God leaves a great deal out. The serpent was a creature that could be used of Satan, and Satan used him. Isn't that exactly the method that Satan uses today? Paul wrote to the Corinthians: "And no marvel; for Satan himself is transformed into an angel of light" (2 Cor. 11:14). The Book of Revelation says more about Satan than anywhere else in Scripture. "And the great dragon was cast out, that old serpent, called the Devil, and Satan, which deceiveth the whole world: he was cast out into the earth, and his angels were cast out with him" (Rev. 12:9). This creature was not a slithering snake as we think of it today. That is not the picture that the Word of God gives of him at all. "And he laid hold on the dragon, that old serpent, which is the Devil, and Satan, and bound him a thousand years" (Rev. 20:2).

This is a creature with tremendous ability. There is no record of his origin here in Genesis at all. I believe that Isaiah 14 and Ezekiel 28 give us the origin of this creature and also how he became the creature that he was.

And the woman said unto the serpent, We may eat of the fruit of the trees of the garden:

But of the fruit of the tree which is in the midst of the garden, God hath said, Ye shall not eat of it, neither shall ye touch it, lest ye die [Gen. 3:2–3].

Why in the world did the serpent approach the woman? Why didn't he approach the man? When God created Adam, He had told him that he could eat of every tree of the garden, but of this one he was not to eat. Woman was created last, and she had gotten her information secondhand; she had gotten it from man. And so the serpent approached woman first. Frankly, I think that woman was created finer than man; that is, she had more compassion and sympathy in her makeup. She was probably more open to suggestion than the man. Actually, I think a woman has a nature that is more inquisitive than a man's. She is the one today who goes into the cults and isms more than anyone else and leads men into them. In fact, many of the founders of cults and isms have been women.

Satan knew what he was doing. Notice what he did. He had a very subtle method as he came. He asked her this question, which cast doubt on the Word of God, "Yea, hath God said, Ye shall not eat of every tree of the garden?" He raises a doubt in her mind and excites her curiosity. She answers, "We can eat of all the trees, but this tree God has told us, 'Ye shall not eat of it [that's all God had said, but she added something], neither shall ye touch it, lest ye die.'" I do not find where He ever said, "You are not to touch it."

THE SERPENT DENIES THE WORD OF GOD

And the serpent said unto the woman, Ye shall not surely die:

For God doth know that in the day ye eat thereof, then your eyes shall be opened, and ye shall be as gods, knowing good and evil [Gen. 3:4-5].

Instead of saying, "Ye shall not surely die," what he said in effect was, "Ye *certainly* shall not die. Why, that is just absolutely impossible!" He questions the love of God and the goodness of God: "If God is good, why did He put this restriction down?" The serpent implies that God is not righteous when he says, "You will not die." And he questions the holiness of God by saying, "You're going to be gods yourselves, for God doth know that in the day ye eat thereof, then your eyes shall be opened, and ye shall be as gods, knowing good and evil."

The thing that Eve did was to add to the Word of God. The liberal and the atheist take *from* the Word of God, and God has warned against that. The cults (and some fundamentalists, by the way) *add* to the Word of God, and God warns against that. There are those who say that today we are saved by law. They argue, "Yes, it is by faith, but it is faith plus something else"—and they are apt to come up with anything. The Word of God says: "Jesus answered and said unto them, This is the work of God, that ye believe on him whom he hath sent" (John 6:29). How important this is!

The serpent very subtly contradicts God, and he substitutes his word for God's word. The Book of Romans teaches the fact of the obedience of faith. Faith leads to obedience, and unbelief leads to disobedience. Doubt leads to disobedience—always.

THE MAN AND WOMAN DISOBEY
THE WORD OF GOD

And when the woman saw that the tree was good for food, and that it was pleasant to the eyes, and a tree to be desired to make one wise, she took of the fruit thereof, and did eat, and gave also unto her husband with her; and he did eat [Gen. 3:6].

Notice that the appeal the serpent made is quite an interesting one. It was an appeal to the flesh—"the tree was good for food"—but that is not all; that is not the thing that is really important. "It was pleasant to the eyes"—it was an appeal to the psychological part of man, to his mind. "And a tree to be desired to make one wise"—this is an appeal to the religious side of man.

You will find that this is the exact temptation that Satan brought to the Lord Jesus in the wilderness (see Matt. 4, Mark 1, and Luke 4). First of all, he said to our Lord, "Make these stones into bread"—this was the appeal to the flesh, as the tree was good for food. Then Satan showed the Lord the kingdoms of the world and offered them to Him—that was an appeal to the mind, as the tree was pleasant to the eyes. Then finally he said, "Cast Yourself down from the temple"—this was an appeal to the religious side of man, as the tree was to be desired to make one wise. I do not think that the Devil has changed his tactics today. He uses the same tactics with you and me, and the reason that he still uses them is that they work. He hasn't needed to change his tactics, for we all seem to fall for the same line.

John wrote: "For all that is in the world, the lust of the flesh, and the lust of the eyes, and the pride of life, is not of the Father, but is of the world" (1 John 2:16). "The lust of the flesh"—that is, the tree was good to eat. "The lust of the eyes"—the tree was good to look at. "The pride of life"—the tree was to be desired to make one wise. These things are not of the Father, but of the world. Jesus said that these sins of the flesh come out of the heart of man, way down deep. This is where Satan is making his appeal. This is the method that he is using in order that he might reach in and lead mankind astray. And he succeeded. They were told that they would know good and evil—and what happened? We now have the results of the fall of man.

And the eyes of them both were opened, and they knew that they were naked; and they sewed fig leaves together, and made themselves aprons [Gen. 3:7].

"And the eyes of them both were opened"—this refers to their conscience. Before the fall, man did not have a conscience; he was innocent. Innocence is ignorance of evil. Man did not make conscience. It is an accuser that each one of us has living on the inside of us. A leading psychologist in a university in Southern California, who is a Christian, said to me that the guilt complex is as much a part of man as his right arm is. Man *cannot* get rid of that guilt complex in a psychological way.

"And they knew that they were naked; and they sewed fig leaves together, and made themselves aprons." Have you ever noticed that the fig tree is the only tree that is specifically mentioned? (The tree of the knowledge of good and evil is not an apple tree. I do not know what it was, but I am almost sure it was not an apple tree.) These fig leaves concealed but did not really cover. Adam and Eve did not confess; they just attempted to cover up their sin. They were not ready to admit their lost condition.

This is the same condition of man today in religion. He goes through exercises and rituals, he joins churches, and he becomes very religious. Have you ever noticed that Christ cursed the fig tree? That is quite interesting. And He denounced religion right after that, by the way; He denounced it with all His being because religion merely covers over sin.

In this temptation Satan wanted to come between man's soul and God. In other words, he wanted to wean man from God, to win man over to himself, and to become the god of man. The temptations of the flesh would not have appealed to man in that day, anyway. He was not tempted to steal or lie or covet. He was just tempted to doubt God. What was the trouble with the rich young ruler? He did not believe God. In the parable of the tares, the tares are those who would not believe God. Notice Satan's method. First, Eve saw that the tree was good for food; second, it was pleasant to the eye; and third, it was to be desired to make one wise. Satan works from the outside to the inside, from without to within.

On the other hand, God begins with man's heart. Religion is something that you rub on the outside, but God does not begin with religion. May I make a distinction here: Christianity is not a religion; Christianity is Christ. There are a lot of religions, but the Lord Jesus went right to the fountainhead when He said, "Ye must be born again."

He said to the Pharisees who were very religious on the outside, "Make the inside of the platter clean. You are just like a mausoleum, beautiful on the outside with marble and flowers, but inside full of dead men's bones." What a picture! And Adam and Eve, instead of confessing their sin, sewed fig leaves together as a covering. May I say to you, there is really no new style in fig leaves. Men are still going to church and going through religious exercises and good works instead of confessing the sin of their hearts.

> **And they heard the voice of the LORD God walking in the garden in the cool of the day: and Adam and his wife hid themselves from the presence of the LORD God amongst the trees of the garden.**

> **And the LORD God called unto Adam, and said unto him, Where art thou? [Gen. 3:8–9].**

Religion will *separate* you from God—and Adam is lost. Adam is lost, and it is God seeking him and not man seeking God.

> **And he said, I heard thy voice in the garden, and I was afraid, because I was naked; and I hid myself.**

> **And he said, Who told thee that thou wast naked? Hast thou eaten of the tree, whereof I commanded thee that thou shouldest not eat?**

> **And the man said, The woman whom thou gavest to be with me, she gave me of the tree, and I did eat [Gen. 3:10–12].**

Notice that there is no confession on Adam's part. The important thing is not so much that he blamed the woman or, as we would say in the common colloquialism of the day, "he passed the buck," but that there is no confession of sin on his part.

> **And the LORD God said unto the woman, What is this that thou hast done? And the woman said, The serpent beguiled me, and I did eat [Gen. 3:13].**

Here is some more of that so-called "buck passing."

THE DESIGN OF GOD FOR THE FUTURE

This man, this creature that God has made, has now turned aside from God, and God must deal with him and must judge him.

> **And the LORD God said unto the serpent, Because thou hast done this, thou art cursed above all cattle, and above every beast of the field; upon thy belly shalt thou go, and dust shalt thou eat all the days of thy life [Gen. 3:14].**

The serpent is certainly not the slithering creature that we think of today. He was different at the beginning, and there has now been pronounced upon him this judgment from God. God pronounces a judgment upon Satan which has a tremendous effect upon man. I would urge you to memorize the following verse, for this is one that you certainly ought to know. This verse is the first prophecy of the coming of the Messiah, the Savior, into the world:

And I will put enmity between thee and the woman, and between thy seed and her seed; it shall bruise thy head, and thou shalt bruise his heel [Gen. 3:15].

"And I will put enmity between thee [that is, Satan] and the woman, and between thy seed and her seed; it [that is, Christ] shall bruise thy head, and thou shalt bruise his heel." This is a tremendous statement that is given to us here. The most prominent thought is not the ultimate victory that would come, but the long-continued struggle. This verse reveals the fact that now there is to be a long struggle between good and evil. This is exactly what you will find in the rest of the Scriptures. The Lord Jesus made this statement in His day concerning this struggle: "Ye are of your father the devil, and the lusts of your father ye will do. He was a murderer from the beginning, and abode not in the truth, because there is no truth in him. When he speaketh a lie, he speaketh of his own: for he is a liar, and the father of it" (John 8:44). "The devil" is Satan. The Lord Jesus Christ made the distinction between children of God and children of Satan. John again mentions this conflict in 1 John 3:10: "In this the children of God are manifest, and the children of the devil: whosoever doeth not righteousness is not of God, neither he that loveth not his brother." Thus we have brought before us the fact that here is a conflict, here is a struggle, and here are two seeds in the world. There will be the final victory—but the long-continued struggle is important to note. Every man must face temptation and must win his battle. Before Christ came, the victory was through obedience in faith. After Christ came, we are to identify ourselves with Christ through faith. What does it mean to be saved? It means to be *in Christ*.

Man was one of three orders of creation: angels, man, and animals. Animals were given no choice, but man and angels were given a choice. Here you have, if you please, man's choice. He has made a decision, and he is held responsible for the decision that he has made.

Notice that it says "her seed." It does not say the man's seed. Here is at least the suggestion of the virgin birth of Christ. When God went into that garden looking for man, He said, "Where art thou?" Any anthology of religion tells the story of man's search for God. My friend, that is not the way God tells it. Let's tell it like it is: Salvation is God's search for man. Man ran away from Him, and God called to him, "Where art thou?" Dr. W. H. Griffith Thomas in his book, Genesis, A Devotional Commentary, makes the comment that "it is the call of Divine justice, which cannot overlook sin. It is the call of Divine sorrow, which grieves over the sinner. It is the call of Divine love, which offers redemption for sin." We have all of that in the verse before us—the promise of the coming of the Savior.

God's search for man is pictured all the way through Scripture. Paul wrote, ". . . there is none that seeketh after God" (Rom. 3:11). The Lord Jesus said, "Ye have not chosen me, but I have chosen you . . ." (John 15:16). And we can say with John, "We love him, because he first loved us" (1 John 4:19). God seeks out man, and He offers man salvation, but there is going to be a long struggle that will take place.

> **Unto the woman he said, I will greatly multiply thy sorrow and thy conception; in sorrow thou shalt bring forth children; and thy desire shall be to thy husband, and he shall rule over thee [Gen. 3:16].**

This is the judgment upon woman. She cannot bring a child into the world without sorrow. Isn't it interesting that that should be true? The very thing that brings joy into the life and continues the human family has to come through sorrow.

> **And unto Adam he said, Because thou hast harkened unto the voice of thy wife, and hast eaten of the tree, of which I commanded thee, saying, Thou shalt not eat of it: cursed is the ground for thy sake; in sorrow shalt thou eat of it all the days of thy life;**

> Thorns also and thistles shall it bring forth to thee; and
> thou shalt eat the herb of the field:
>
> In the sweat of thy face shalt thou eat bread, till thou
> return unto the ground; for out of it wast thou taken: for
> dust thou art, and unto dust shalt thou return [Gen.
> 3:17–19].

This is the judgment upon man. Death now comes to man. What is death? Physical death is a separation of the person, the spirit, the soul, from the body. Ecclesiastes says: "Then shall the dust return to the earth as it was: and the spirit shall return unto God who gave it" (Eccl. 12:7). Man ultimately must answer to God. Whether he is saved or lost, he is going to have to answer to God. But Adam did not die physically the day that he ate. He did not die until more than nine hundred years later. The whole point is simply this: he died *spiritually* the moment he disobeyed; he was separated from God. Death is separation. When Paul wrote to the Ephesians that they were "dead in trespasses and sins," he did not mean that they were dead physically but that they were dead spiritually, separated from God. In that wonderful parable of the prodigal son, our Lord told about this boy who ran away from his father. When he returned, the father said to the elder son, "For this my son was dead, and is alive again; he was lost, and is found . . ." (Luke 15:24). Dead? Yes, he was dead, not physically, but he was separated from the father. To be separated from the Father means simply that—it means death. The Lord Jesus said to Martha, ". . . I am the resurrection, and the life: he that believeth in me, though he were dead, yet shall he live" (John 11:25). Again, "dead" means death spiritually, that is, separation from God. Man died spiritually the moment he ate. That is the reason he ran away from God. That is the reason he sewed fig leaves for a covering.

THE DOCTRINE OF REDEMPTION INTRODUCED

> And Adam called his wife's name Eve; because she was
> the mother of all living [Gen. 3:20].

This does not mean that Cain and Abel were born in the Garden of Eden, but it is definite that they were born *after* the fall of Adam and Eve.

Unto Adam also and to his wife did the LORD God make coats of skins, and clothed them [Gen. 3:21].

In order to have the skins of animals, the animals have to be slain. I believe that this is the origin of sacrifice and that God made it clear to man. God rejected their fig leaves but made them clothing of skins, and when Adam and Eve left the Garden of Eden, they looked back upon a bloody sacrifice. When they looked back, they saw exactly what God had Moses put on the mercy seat in the Holy of Holies: two cherubim looking down upon the blood that was there—and that was the way to God.

There are four great lessons that we see from the fig leaves and the fact that God clothed them with skins. (1) Man must have adequate covering to approach God. You cannot come to God on the basis of your good works. You must come just as you are—a sinner. (2) Fig leaves are unacceptable; they are homemade. God does not take a homemade garment. (3) God must provide the covering. (4) The covering is obtained only through the death of the Lord Jesus.

Man must have a substitute between himself and God's wrath. That is important even in these days for man to consider. The hardest thing in the world is for man to take his rightful position before God. This anonymous poem on prayer reveals the necessity of this even in our own hearts:

> He prayed for strength that he might achieve;
> He was made weak that he might obey.
> He prayed for health that he might do greater things;
> He was given infirmity that he might do better things;
> He prayed for riches that he might be happy;
> He was given poverty that he might be wise.
> He prayed for power that he might have the praise of
>   men;

He was given infirmity that he might feel the need of
    God.
He prayed for all things that he might enjoy life;
He was given life that he might enjoy all things.
He had received nothing that he asked for—all that he
    hoped for;
His prayer was answered—he was most blessed.

Salvation comes when you and I take our proper place as sinners before God.

**And the Lord God said, Behold, the man is become as
one of us, to know good and evil: and now, lest he put
forth his hand, and take also of the tree of life, and eat,
and live for ever:**

**Therefore the Lord God sent him forth from the garden
of Eden, to till the ground from whence he was taken
[Gen. 3:22–23].**

All I can say to this is, thank God that He did not let man live eternally in sin and that God is not going to let us do that. That is really a blessing!

**So he drove out the man; and he placed at the east of the
garden of Eden Cherubims, and a flaming sword which
turned every way, to keep the way of the tree of life [Gen.
3:24].**

This does not mean that God put up a roadblock. It means that the way of life was kept open for man to come to God. But now that way is not through the tree of life. Salvation must come through a sacrifice, and when man looked back, the blood of the sacrifice is what he saw.

CHAPTER 4

THEME: The birth of Cain and Abel; God gives Cain a
second chance; Cain murders Abel; the children of
Cain and a godless civilization; the birth of Seth

In Genesis 3 we have the *root* of sin and in Genesis 4 the *fruit* of sin.
How bad is sin? Well, in this chapter, we find that man was not just
suffering from ptomaine poisoning because of having eaten the fruit
of the tree of knowledge of good and evil. Chapter 4 reveals how much
had really happened to the man. By his disbelief and his disobedience, he had turned away from God and had sinned in such a way that
he brought upon himself and his race His judgment, because you and
I are given this same kind of nature. We have the same nature that our
father had, and Adam has given all of us a pretty bad nature. All this is
revealed in the story of the two sons of Adam and Eve. They had more
children than this, but we are given the record of only these two at this
time.

THE BIRTH OF CAIN AND ABEL

**And Adam knew Eve his wife; and she conceived, and
bare Cain, and said, I have gotten a man from the LORD
[Gen. 4:1].**

This reveals the fact that Adam and Eve certainly did not anticipate
that the struggle was going to be long. When Cain was born, Eve must
have said, "I have gotten the man from the Lord. God said that the
seed of the woman would bruise the head of the serpent—and here he
is!" But Cain was not the one. He was a murderer, he was no savior at
all. It will be a long time before the Savior comes. For a minimum of
six thousand years—and I think it has been longer than that—the
struggle has been going on between the seed of the woman and the
seed of the serpent.

> **And she again bare his brother Abel. And Abel was a keeper of sheep, but Cain was a tiller of the ground [Gen. 4:2].**

These are the two boys that we are looking at.

> **And in process of time it came to pass, that Cain brought of the fruit of the ground an offering unto the LORD [Gen. 4:3].**

"In process of time" actually means "at the end of days," which would mean on the Sabbath Day, on the day that God had rested.

"Cain brought"—the idea of "brought" means to an appointed place. They are bringing an offering to God to an appointed place to worship. All this would indicate that they are doing it by revelation. I *know* that they are, for when we turn to Hebrews 11:4, we read: "By faith Abel offered unto God a more excellent sacrifice than Cain, by which he obtained witness that he was righteous, God testifying of his gifts: and by it he being dead yet speaketh." How could Abel offer it "by faith"? "So then faith cometh by hearing, and hearing by the word of God" (Rom. 10:17). God had to have given His Word about this, or this boy Abel could never have come by faith, and that is the way he came. The other boy did not come that way. "Cain brought of the fruit of the ground." There is nothing wrong with the fruit. Don't think that he brought the leftovers—his attitude is not that of giving old clothes to the mission. I think that the fruit he brought would have won the blue ribbon in any county or state fair in the country. He brought the best of his beautiful, delicious fruit, and he brought it as an offering to the Lord.

> **And Abel, he also brought of the firstlings of his flock and of the fat thereof. And the LORD had respect unto Abel and to his offering:**
>
> **But unto Cain and to his offering he had not respect. And Cain was very wroth, and his countenance fell [Gen. 4:4–5].**

Someone may say, "I don't see anything *wrong* in the thing Cain did." In the eleventh verse of his epistle, speaking of apostates in the last days, Jude says, ". . . They have gone in the way of Cain . . ." What is the way of Cain? When Cain brought an offering to God, he did not come by faith—he came on his own. And the offering that he brought denied that human nature is evil. God said, "Bring that little blood sacrifice which will point to the Redeemer who is coming into the world. Come on that basis, and don't come by bringing the works of your own hands."

Cain's offering also denied that man was separated from God. He acted like everything was all right. This is what liberalism does today in talking about the universal fatherhood of God and the universal brotherhood of man. My friend, things are *not* all right with us today. We are *not* born children of God. We have to be born *again* to be children of God. Man is separated from God. Cain refused to recognize that, and multitudes today refuse to do so.

The third thing that Cain's offering denied was that man cannot offer works to God—Cain felt he could. Scripture says: "Not by works of righteousness which we have done, but according to his mercy he saved us, by the washing of regeneration, and renewing of the Holy Ghost" (Titus 3:5). The difference between Cain and Abel was not a character difference at all, but the difference was in the offerings which they brought. These two boys had the same background. They had the same heredity. They had the same environment. There was not that difference between them. Don't tell me that Cain got his bad disposition from an alcoholic grandfather on his father's side—he didn't have a grandfather. And don't say that Abel got his good disposition from a very fine grandmother on his mother's side. They just didn't have grandparents. They had the same heredity and the same environment. The difference was in the offerings.

That offering makes a difference in men today. No Christian takes the position that he is better than anyone else. The thing that makes him a Christian is that he recognizes that he is a sinner like everyone else and that he needs an offering, he needs a sacrifice, and he needs Someone to take his place and to die for him. Paul says of Christ: "Whom God hath set forth to be a propitiation through faith in his blood . . ." (Rom. 3:25). Therefore Paul could further write: "For they being ignorant of God's righteousness, and going about to establish their own righteousness, have not submitted themselves unto the righteousness of God" (Rom. 10:3). That is the picture of multitudes of people today. They are attempting through religion, through joining a church and doing something, to make themselves acceptable to God. God's righteousness can only come to you—because it must be a *perfect* righteousness—through Christ's providing it for you. "Who was delivered for our offences, and was raised again for our justification" (Rom. 4:25). That is, He was raised for our righteousness. He was the One who took our place. "For he hath made him to be sin for us, who knew no sin; that we might be made the righteousness of God in him" (2 Cor. 5:21). Paul says in Philippians 3:8-9, ". . . That I may win Christ, And be found in him, not having mine own righteousness, which is of the law, but that which is through the faith of Christ. . . ." The righteousness of Cain was his own righteousness. The righteousness of Abel was faith in a sacrifice that looked forward to Christ's sacrifice.

We have seen that Cain and Abel had come together to worship God. These two boys were identical. Some expositors actually believe they were twins—I think that was the position of the late Dr. Harry Rimmer. But I believe they were even closer than twins because of the fact they had no blood stream which reached way back on both sides that might cause a difference. They were the sons of Adam and Eve. However, there is a great divergence between Cain and Abel which is not necessarily a character divergence. One was accepted because of the sacrifice which he brought by faith; the other, Cain, brought his offering without any recognition from God at all.

GOD GIVES CAIN A SECOND CHANCE

And the LORD said unto Cain, Why art thou wroth? and why is thy countenance fallen?

If thou doest well, shalt thou not be accepted? and if thou doest not well, sin lieth at the door. And unto thee

shall be his desire, and thou shalt rule over him [Gen. 4:6–7].

Why is Cain angry? He is angry enough that he is going to slay his brother. Back of premeditated murder there always is anger. Our Lord said that, if you are angry with your brother without a cause, you are guilty of murder. Back of anger is jealousy, and back of jealousy is pride. There is no sense of sin whatsoever in spiritual pride. James put it in language like this: "Then when lust hath conceived, it bringeth forth sin: and sin, when it is finished, bringeth forth death" (James 1:15). Cain's anger led to murder, but back of that was his jealousy and also his pride.

And that is how God deals with him. He says to Cain, "If thou doest well, shalt thou not be accepted?" Actually, the meaning is better translated as, "Shalt thou not have excellency?" The eldest son always occupied a place of preeminence, and this boy thinks that now he will lose that. God tells him there is no reason for him to lose it if he does well. To do well would be to bring that which God had accepted from Abel, a sacrifice and the acknowledgment that he was a sinner. But not this boy—he's just angry.

"Sin lieth at the door." There are those who have interpreted this as meaning that a sin offering lies at the door; that is, that there is the little lamb lying at the door. That makes sense because that was true, but I do not think it means the sin offering here. Up to this time and beyond this time, in fact, up until Moses, as far as I can tell from the Word of God, there was no sin offering. You find the instructions given for the sin offering in the Book of Leviticus. In the first part of that book, five offerings are given, and one is the sin offering. the sin offering did not come into existence until the law was given. That is the thing that Paul is saying in Romans 3:20: ". . . For by the law is the knowledge of sin." The offerings that were brought up to that time were burnt offerings. Job in his day, which obviously was before Moses, brought a burnt offering. It was not in any way a sin offering. I think if you will examine the Scriptures, you will find that that is true.

It is obvious that Cain did not realize how vulnerable to sin he was.

When God said to him that "sin lieth at the door," I believe He was saying that sin, like a wild beast, was crouching at the door waiting to pounce on him the moment he stepped out. For that reason Cain needed a sacrifice that would be acceptable to God for sin, a sacrifice that pointed to Christ. "Not as Cain, who was of that wicked one, and slew his brother. And wherefore slew he him? Because his own works were evil, and his brother's righteous" (1 John 3:12). "If thou doest not well, sin lieth at the door." To do well would have been to bring the kind of offering that Abel had brought, a burnt offering. You find that Abraham also offered a burnt offering, for there could be no transgression until the law was given; that is, sin would not become a trespass against law until then. Therefore, you find that God actually protected this man Cain.

CAIN MURDERS ABEL

And Cain talked with Abel his brother: and it came to pass, when they were in the field, that Cain rose up against Abel his brother, and slew him.

And the LORD said unto Cain, Where is Abel thy brother? And he said, I know not: Am I my brother's keeper? [Gen. 4:8–9].

This is practically an impudent answer. He frankly had little regard for either his brother or for his God. He is trying to cover his action, but the Scriptures say, ". . . there is nothing covered, that shall not be revealed; and hid, that shall not be known" (Matt. 10:26). That is something to think over if you have any secret sins. You had better deal with them down here because they are all going to come out in God's presence someday anyway. He already knows about them—you might just as well tell Him about them. This fellow Cain tries to say that he is not guilty. "Am I my brother's keeper?"—what an impudent answer!

And he said, What hast thou done? the voice of thy brother's blood crieth unto me from the ground [Gen. 4:10].

The writer to the Hebrews uses this in Hebrews 12:24: "And to Jesus the mediator of the new covenant, and to the blood of sprinkling, that speaketh better things than that of Abel." Abel's blood spoke of murder committed. The blood of Christ speaks of redemption; it speaks of salvation.

And now art thou cursed from the earth, which hath opened her mouth to receive thy brother's blood from thy hand;

When thou tillest the ground, it shall not henceforth yield unto thee her strength; a fugitive and a vagabond shalt thou be in the earth [Gen. 4:11–12].

Yet in our day there is a curse upon the earth because of man's sin which causes it to lose its fertility. In some of the most lush sections of our earth multitudes of folk are starving. It takes great effort and ingenuity for man to make this earth produce in abundance. Certainly the blood of Abel cries out from the very earth itself—blood that was spilled in murder by a brother.

And Cain said unto the Lord, My punishment is greater than I can bear [Gen. 4:13].

If Cain's punishment was greater than he could bear, why didn't he just turn to God and confess his sin and cast himself upon God's mercy? It *was* too great for him to bear, but God was providing a Savior for him if he would only turn to Him.

Behold, thou hast driven me out this day from the face of the earth; and from thy face shall I be hid; and I shall be

> **a fugitive and a vagabond in the earth; and it shall come to pass, that every one that findeth me shall slay me [Gen. 4:14].**

Cain says now that he is to be hidden from the face of God, and of course, that is exactly what happened.

But notice now that God protects him. This is strange: God is actually harboring a murderer, a criminal.

> **And the LORD said unto him, Therefore whosoever slayeth Cain, vengeance shall be taken on him sevenfold. And the LORD set a mark upon Cain, lest any finding him should kill him [Gen. 4:15].**

I do not know what the mark was. There has been a lot of speculation, and I do not know why I should add my speculation to all of it. But God protects Cain. There has been no law given at this time. Cain is a sinner, but he is not a transgressor because there has been no law given about murder. His great sin is that he did not bring the offering that was acceptable to God. His deeds were evil in what he brought to God, and he manifested that evil nature in slaying his brother.

THE CHILDREN OF CAIN AND
A GODLESS CIVILIZATION

We find that Cain moves out from God, and he establishes a civilization that is apart from God altogether. The children of Cain establish a godless civilization.

> **And Cain went out from the presence of the LORD, and dwelt in the land of Nod, on the east of Eden [Gen. 4:16].**

I know a lot of folk who dwell in "the land of nod" when they are in church, but frankly, I do not know where the land of Nod really is. I have often wondered just where it is, and again, there is speculation about this. But we are told that Cain went out and dwelt in that area.

> **And Cain knew his wife; and she conceived, and bare Enoch: and he builded a city, and called the name of the city, after the name of his son, Enoch [Gen. 4:17].**

Men have been doing this ever since. They like to call streets and cities by their own names or by names of loved ones. Even in Christian work you have schools named for individuals. Men love to do that, whether they are Christian or whether they are after the order of Cain.

But here is where urban life, city life, began: "and he builded a city, and called the name of the city, after the name of his son, Enoch." Cities have become one of the biggest problems that man has today. The cities, they say, are dying, and yet people all over the world are flocking to the cities.

> **And unto Enoch was born Irad: and Irad begat Mehujael: and Mehujael begat Methuselah: and Methuselah begat Lamech.**
>
> **And Lamech took unto him two wives: the name of the one was Adah, and the name of the other Zillah [Gen. 4:18–19].**

Here is the beginning of polygamy—having more than one wife. Lamech now does that which is contrary to what God intends, contrary to what God has for man. You will never find anywhere in the Scriptures that God approves of polygamy. If you read the accounts accurately, you will find that He condemns it. He gives the record of it because He is giving a *historical* record, and that is the basis on which it is given to us here.

"Adah" means *pleasure* or *adornment*. She was the first one to make it to the beauty parlor, I guess. "Zillah" means *to hide*; I suppose that means she was a coquette. My, what two girls he had for wives! No wonder he had problems. Later on we will see what happened.

Here now is the beginning of civilization, the Cainitic civilization.

> **And Adah bare Jabal: he was the father of such as dwell in tents, and of such as have cattle [Gen. 4:20].**

"He was the father of such as dwell in tents." The apostle Paul was a tentmaker later on, but here is the first housing contractor. "And of such as have cattle"—here was the first rancher.

> **And his brother's name was Jubal: he was the father of all such as handle the harp and organ [Gen. 4:21].**

Here is the beginning of the musicians. When we hear some of the modern music today, I am sure there are many who would agree that it must have begun with Cain's civilization!

> **And Zillah, she also bare Tubal-cain, an instructor of every artificer in brass and iron: and the sister of Tubal-cain was Naamah [Gen. 4:22].**

Here we see the ones who are craftsmen.

> **And Lamech said unto his wives, Adah and Zillah, Hear my voice; ye wives of Lamech, hearken unto my speech: for I have slain a man to my wounding, and a young man to my hurt.**
>
> **If Cain shall be avenged sevenfold, truly Lamech seventy and sevenfold [Gen. 4:23–24].**

Lamech says, "If Cain got by with it, I can get by with it. After all, Cain did not slay in self-defense, but I have." I do not know whether he did or not, but he says that he slew in self-defense. And I do not know whether or not his two wives entered into this, or whether or not he was defending one of them. We are not told how it happened. Lamech feels that he will be *avenged* seventy and sevenfold, but our Lord told Simon Peter that he ought to *forgive* his enemy that many times.

THE BIRTH OF SETH

And Adam knew his wife again; and she bare a son, and called his name Seth: For God, said she, hath appointed me another seed instead of Abel, whom Cain slew.

And to Seth, to him also there was born a son; and he called his name Enos: then began men to call upon the name of the Lord [Gen. 4:25–26].

Apparently this was the beginning of men calling upon the name of the Lord.

CHAPTER 5

THEME: Final chapter of Adam's biography; the thrilling story of Enoch; the genealogy of Enoch to Noah

In the first section of the Book of Genesis (chapters 1—11), we have world events—first the Creation, then the Fall, and now the Flood in chapters 5—9. In chapter 5 we have the book of the generations of Adam through Seth. Cain's line has been given to us and is now dropped. It will be mentioned again only as it crosses the godly line. This is a pattern that will be set in the Book of Genesis.

In one sense, chapter 5 is one of the most discouraging and despondent chapters in the Bible. The reason is simply that it is like walking through a cemetery. God said to Adam, ". . . For in the day that thou eatest thereof thou shalt surely die" (Gen. 2:17), and they all died who were the sons of Adam. Paul says, "For as in Adam all die . . ." (1 Cor. 15:22).

FINAL CHAPTER OF ADAM'S BIOGRAPHY

This is the book of the generations of Adam. In the day that God created man, in the likeness of God made he him;

Male and female created he them; and blessed them, and called their name Adam, in the day when they were created [Gen. 5:1–2].

"And blessed them, and called their name Adam"—not the Adamses, but Adam. He called *their* name Adam—Eve is the other half of him.

"The book of the generations of Adam." This strange expression occurs again only in the beginning of the New Testament, and there it is "the book of the generation of Jesus Christ." There are these two books, as we are already seeing that there are two lines, two seeds, and they are against each other. The struggle is going to be long between the line of Satan and the line of Christ, the accepted line. The line which we are following now is the line through Seth, and it is through this line that Christ will ultimately come.

And Adam lived an hundred and thirty years, and begat a son in his own likeness, after his image; and called his name Seth [Gen. 5:3].

When Adam was 130 years old, how old was he? In other words, when God created Adam, did He create him thirty years old or fourteen or forty-five? I do not know—anything would be speculation. And if He created him that old, *was* he that old? And of course God could create him any age. May I say, this answers a lot of questions about the age of the earth. When someone says that certain rocks are billions of years old, they just do not know. Maybe when God created them, He created them two or three billion years old. The important thing here is that when Adam had been here 130 years, he begat a son in *his* own likeness. Adam was made in the likeness of God, but his son was born in his likeness.

And the days of Adam after he had begotten Seth were eight hundred years: and he begat sons and daughters:

And all the days that Adam lived were nine hundred and thirty years: and he died [Gen. 5:4–5].

Now we start through the graveyard. Adam begat sons and daughters, "and all the days that Adam lived were nine hundred and thirty years"—and what happened? "And he died."

In verse 8 we read what happened to Seth. He died. He had a son by the name of Enos, and what happened to him? In verse 11 we are told that he died. But he had a son, and Cainan was his son. And what happened to old Cainan? In verse 14 we find that he died too. He had a son, Mahalaleel, and what happened to him? In verse 17 it says he died. But he had a son, and his name was Jared, and, well, he died too (v. 20).

THE THRILLING STORY OF ENOCH

But before he died, Jared had a son by the name of Enoch.

> **And Enoch lived sixty and five years, and begat Methuselah [Gen. 5:21].**

And then did Enoch die? No! He did not die. This is a dark chapter, but here is the bright spot in it.

> **And Enoch walked with God after he begat Methuselah three hundred years, and begat sons and daughters:**
>
> **And all the days of Enoch were three hundred sixty and five years:**
>
> **And Enoch walked with God: and he was not; for God took him [Gen. 5:22–24].**

This is one of the most remarkable things, that in the midst of death one man is removed from this earth. It is said of Enoch that he "walked with God." This is quite remarkable, by the way. Only two men are said to have walked with God. In the next chapter, we find that Noah also walked with God. These were two antediluvians, and they walked with God. There are actually only two men in the Old Testament who did not die. One of them is Enoch, and the other, of course, is Elijah.

Enoch is one of the few before the Flood of whom we have any record at all. We are told that he did not die but that God took him—he was translated. What do we mean by *translation*? Translation is the taking of a word from one language and putting it into another language without changing its meaning. Enoch was removed from this earth; he was translated. He had to get rid of the old body which he had. He had to be a different individual—yet he had to be the same individual, just as the translated word has to be the same. Enoch was taken to heaven.

We read that Enoch lived sixty-five years, and begat Methuselah, and after that he walked with God. I do not know what the first sixty-five years of his life were. I assume that he was like the rest of the crowd—this was a very careless period, moving now into the orbit of the days of Noah. But when that little boy Methuselah was born, Enoch's walk was changed. That baby turned him to God. My friend, sometimes God puts a baby in a family just for that purpose, and if that baby will not bring you to God, nothing else will. For three hundred years after that he walked with God, and he begat other children, sons and daughters. "And all the days of Enoch were three hundred sixty and five years"—that is how long he was on this earth, but he did not die. It does not say, "And then Enoch died," but it says, "And Enoch walked with God: and he *was* not; for God took him."

The only way I know to describe this is the way a little girl described it to her mother when she came home from Sunday school. She said, "Teacher told us about Enoch and how he walked with God." Her mother said, "Well, what about Enoch?" And the little girl put it something like this: "It seems that every day God would come by and say to Enoch, 'Enoch, would you like to walk with Me?' And Enoch would come out of his house and down to the gate, and he'd go walking with God. He got to the place that he enjoyed it so much that he'd be waiting at the gate of his house every day. And God would come along and say, 'Enoch, let's take a walk.' Then one day God came by and said, 'Enoch, let's take a long walk. I have so much to tell you.' So they were walking and walking, and finally Enoch said, 'My, it's getting late in the afternoon, I'd better get back home!' And God said to him, 'Enoch, you're closer to My home than you are to your home; so you come on home with Me.' And so Enoch went home with God." I do not know how you can put it any better than that, my friend. That is exactly the story that is here.

I think that all the great truths here in Genesis are germane. In my judgment, this is the picture of what is to come; here is the Rapture of the church. Before the judgment of the Flood, God removes Enoch.

THE GENEALOGY OF ENOCH TO NOAH

And all the days of Methuselah were nine hundred sixty and nine years: and he died [Gen. 5:27].

GENEALOGY OF THE PATRIARCHS

These Columns Show Which of the Patriarchs Were Contemporary With Each Other

HORIZONTAL LIST → (Adam, Seth, Enos, Cainan, Mahalaleel, Jared, Enoch, Methuselah, Lamech, Noah, Shem, Arphaxad, Salah, Eber, Peleg, Reu, Serug, Nahor, Terah, Abram, Isaac, Jacob)

VERTICAL LIST ↓

Decorative lettering across upper field: **A G E D**

Name		Adam	Seth	Enos	Cainan	Mahalaleel	Jared	Enoch	Methuselah	Lamech	Noah	Shem	Arphaxad	Salah	Eber	Peleg	Reu	Serug	Nahor	Terah	Abram	Isaac	Jacob
Adam	Cr																						
Seth	B	130																					
Enos	B	235	105																				
Cainan	B	325	195	90																			
Mahalaleel	B	395	265	160	70																		
Jared	B	460	330	225	135	65																	
Enoch	B	622	492	387	297	227	162																
Methuselah	B	687	557	452	362	292	227	65															
Lamech	B	874	744	639	549	479	414	252	187														
Adam	D	930	800	695	605	535	470	308	243	56													
Enoch	Tr		857	752	662	592	527	365	300	113													
Seth	D		912	807	717	647	582		355	168													
Noah	B			821	731	661	596		369	182													
Enos	D			905	815	745	680		453	266	84												
Cainan	D				910	840	775		548	361	179												
Mahalaleel	D					895	830		603	416	234												
Jared	D						962		735	548	366												
Shem	B								871	684	502												
Lamech	D								964	777	595	93											
Methuselah	D								969		600	98											
The Deluge											600	98											
Arphaxad	B										602	100											
Salah	B										637	135	35										
Eber	B										667	165	65	30									
Peleg	B										701	199	99	64	34								
Reu	B										731	229	129	94	64	30							
Serug	B										763	261	161	126	96	62	32						
Nahor	B										793	291	191	156	126	92	62	30					
Terah	B										822	320	220	185	155	121	91	59	29				
Abram	B										892	390	290	255	225	191	161	129	99	70			
Peleg	D										940	438	338	303	273	239	209	177	147	118			
Nahor	D										941	439	339	304	274		210	178	148	119			
Noah	D										950	448	348	313	283		219	187		128			
Reu	D											468	368	333	303		239	207		148	18		
Serug	D											491	391	356	326			230		171	41		
Terah	D											525	425	390	360					205	75		
Arphaxad	D											538	438	403	373						88		
Isaac	B											550		415	385						100		
Salah	D											568		433	403						118	18	
Shem	D											600			435						150	50	
Jacob	B														445						160	60	
Abraham	D														460						175	75	15
Eber	D														464							79	19
Isaac	D																					180	120
Jacob	D																						147

Key: Cr—Creation   B—Born   D—Died   Tr—Translated.

EXAMPLE: Noah (vertical list) was born when Methuselah (horizontal list) was 369 years old.

Methuselah lived longer than Adam. These two men, Adam and Methuselah, pretty well bridged the gap between creation and the Flood. According to our genealogy, this man Methuselah could have told Noah everything from the creation of the world. I personally feel that we have a gap in the genealogy given here. We know that in the opening of the New Testament the genealogy that is given of the Lord Jesus leaves out quite a few, and purposely so, because there is an attempt to give it in three equal segments. Certain ones are left out, but you will notice that it follows through accurately. I am sure that this genealogy is accurate, but the important thing is that we may have a gap here that would account for the fact that man has been on this earth a great deal longer than we have supposed. This is something I do not care to go into because it is quite an involved subject. Scripture is not clear right here. Why isn't it? Because God is not anxious to insist upon that. What He is trying to get over to us is the religious, the redemptive, history of mankind on this earth.

The name of Methuselah means "sending forth." Others believe that Methuselah meant: "When he is dead, it shall be sent." What will be sent? The Flood. As long as Methuselah lived, the Flood could not come. The very interesting thing is that according to a chronology of the genealogy of the patriarchs (shown on the preceding page), the year that Methuselah died is the year that the Flood came. "When he is dead, it shall be sent"—that is the meaning of his name.

Why did Methuselah live longer than any other person? God kept him here just to let mankind know that He is patient and merciful. God will also wait for you, my friend—all of your life. Peter speaks of the long-suffering of our God: "Which sometime were disobedient, when once the long-suffering of God waited in the days of Noah, while the ark was a preparing, wherein few, that is, eight souls were saved by water" (1 Pet. 3:20).

As we continue down through the rest of this chapter, each man is mentioned and then his death.

And all the days of Lamech were seven hundred seventy and seven years: and he died.

**And Noah was five hundred years old: and Noah begat
Shem, Ham, and Japheth [Gen. 5:31–32].**

It is the popular theory in the world, blindly accepted by men, and the
conclusion, I think, of all philosophy, that human nature is inherently
and innately good and that it can be improved. The whole program
that is abroad today is that, if we will just try to improve the environment of man and his heredity, he can really be improved. Communism and socialism seek to improve man. Arminianism means that
man can assist in his salvation. Modernism says that man can save
himself. In other words, salvation is sort of a do-it-yourself kit that
God gives to you. Some of the cults tell us that human nature is totally
good and that there is no such thing as sin.

What does God say concerning man? God says that man is totally
evil, totally bad. That is the condition of all of us. "There is none righteous, no, not one" (Rom. 3:10). That is the estimate of the Word of
God. If you will accept God's Word for it, it will give you a truer conception of life today than is given to us by others.

Here is mankind, and we are following a godly line now. Where is
it going to lead? Is it going to lead to a millennium here upon this
earth? Are they going to come to Elysian fields and establish Utopia?
No. The very next chapter tells us that a Flood, a judgment from God,
came upon the earth.

CHAPTER 6

THEME: Cause of the Flood; God's deliverance from the judgment of the Flood; instructions to Noah for building the ark; passengers in the ark

CAUSE OF THE FLOOD

In chapter 6 we see not only the Flood, but also the reason for the judgment of the Flood.

> **And it came to pass, when men began to multiply on the face of the earth, and daughters were born unto them,**
>
> **That the sons of God saw the daughters of men that they were fair; and they took them wives of all which they chose [Gen. 6:1–2].**

This matter of "the sons of God" and "the daughters of men" is something that has caused no end of discussion. There are a great many good men who take the position that "the sons of God" were angels. I personally cannot accept that at all. Most of my teachers taught that the sons of God were angels, and I recognize that a great many of the present-day expositors take that position. However, I cannot accept that view, because, if these were good angels, they would not commit this sin, and evil angels could never be designated as "sons of God." Also, the offspring here were men; they were not monstrosities. I do not know why it is assumed by so many that the offspring were giants. We will look at this more closely when we come to verse 4.

> **And the LORD said, My spirit shall not always strive with man, for that he also is flesh: yet his days shall be an hundred and twenty years [Gen. 6:3].**

We believe that Noah preached for 120 years, and during that time the Spirit of God was striving with men. Peter makes it very clear that it was back in the days of Noah that the Spirit of God was striving with men in order that He might bring them to God—but they would not turn. "For Christ also hath once suffered for sins, the just for the unjust, that he might bring us to God, being put to death in the flesh, but quickened by the Spirit: By which also he went and preached unto the spirits in prison" (1 Pet. 3:18–19). These spirits were in prison when Peter wrote, but they were preached to in the days of Noah. How do we know that? Verse 20 reads: "Which sometime were disobedient, when once the long-suffering of God waited in the days of Noah, while the ark was a preparing, wherein few, that is, eight souls were saved by water." When were they disobedient? During the long-suffering of God in the days of Noah—during those 120 years.

There were giants in the earth in those days; and also after that, when the sons of God came in unto the daughters of men, and they bare children to them, the same became mighty men which were of old, men of renown [Gen. 6:4].

It says, "There were giants in the earth in those days," but it does not say they are the offspring of the sons of God and the daughters of men. It does say this about the offspring: "the same became mighty men which were of old, men of renown." These were not monstrosities; they were men. The record here makes it very clear that the giants were in the earth *before* this took place, and it simply means that these offspring were outstanding individuals.

Humanity has a tremendous capacity. Man is fearfully and wonderfully made—that is a great truth we have lost sight of. This idea that man has come up from some protoplasm out of a garbage can or seaweed is utterly preposterous. It is the belief of some scientists that evolution will be repudiated, and some folk are going to look ridiculous at that time.

Evolution is nothing in the world but a theory as far as science is concerned. Nothing has been conclusive about it. It is a philosophy like any other philosophy, and it can be accepted or rejected. When it is accepted, it certainly leads to some very crazy solutions to the problems of the world, and it has gotten my country into trouble throughout the world. Anyone would think that we are the white knight riding through the world straightening out wrongs. We are wrong on the inside ourselves! I do not know why in this country today we have an intelligentsia in our colleges, our government, our news media, and our military who think they are super, that somehow or another they have arrived. It is the delusion of the hour that men think that they are greater than they really are. Man is suffering from a fall, an awful fall. He is totally depraved today, and until that is taken into consideration, we are in trouble all the way along.

Then what *do* we have here in verse 4? As I see it, Genesis is a book of genealogies—it is a book of the families. The sons of God are the godly line who have come down from Adam through Seth, and the daughters of men belong to the line of Cain. What you have here now is an intermingling and intermarriage of these two lines, until finally the entire line is totally corrupted (well, not totally; there is one exception). That is the picture that is presented to us here.

I recognize, and I want to insist upon it, that many fine expositors take the opposite view that the sons of God are actually angels. If you accept that view, you will be in good company, but I am sure that most of you want to be right and will want to go along with me. Regardless of which view you take, I hope all of us will be friends, because this is merely a matter of interpretation. It does not have anything to do with whether or not you believe the Bible but concerns only the interpretation of the facts of Scripture.

What was the condition on the earth before the Flood? What caused God to bring the judgment of the Flood?

And God saw that the wickedness of man was great in the earth, and that every imagination of the thoughts of his heart was only evil continually [Gen. 6:5].

There are four words here that ought to be emphasized and which I have marked in my Bible. "The wickedness of man was *great*." "*Every*

imagination of the thoughts of his heart was *only* evil." Only evil—
that is all it was—and that "*continually*." These four words reveal the
condition of the human family that was upon the earth.

**And it repented the Lord that he had made man on the
earth, and it grieved him at his heart [Gen. 6:6].**

"And it repented the Lord." What repented the Lord? The corruption
of man repented the Lord. It looks as if God has changed His mind and
intends to remove man from the earth. He probably did just that with a
former creation on the earth. Although it grieved God because of
man's sin, thank God, He did not destroy him.

**And the Lord said, I will destroy man whom I have cre-
ated from the face of the earth; both man, and beast,
and the creeping thing, and the fowls of the air; for it
repenteth me that I have made them [Gen. 6:7].**

It does not mention fish because they are in the water, and He is simply going to send more water.

GOD'S DELIVERANCE FROM THE JUDGMENT
OF THE FLOOD

But Noah found grace in the eyes of the Lord [Gen. 6:8].

And why did Noah find grace?

**These are the generations of Noah: Noah was a just man
and perfect in his generations, and Noah walked with
God [Gen. 6:9].**

Why did God save Noah? Because he walked with God? Yes, but we
are also told: "By faith Noah, being warned of God of things not seen
as yet, moved with fear, prepared an ark to the saving of his house; by
the which he condemned the world, and became heir of the righteous-

ness which is by faith" (Heb. 11:7). It took faith to prepare an ark on dry land when it had not even drizzled! In this same chapter in Hebrews, we are told that it was by faith that Enoch was translated. You see, when the church is taken out of this world, every believer is going because the rapture is for *believers*, and the weakest saint is going out. They are going out because God extends mercy, and we are told that the mercy of God will be demonstrated at that time.

Why the Flood? Why is God going to send the Flood?

The earth also was corrupt before God, and the earth was filled with violence.

And God looked upon the earth, and, behold, it was corrupt; for all flesh had corrupted his way upon the earth [Gen. 6:11–12].

That is, man had corrupted God's way and was going his own way. He had turned from the purpose for which God had created him.

And God said unto Noah, The end of all flesh is come before me; for the earth is filled with violence through them; and, behold, I will destroy them with the earth [Gen. 6:13].

God is going to send the Flood, and I would like to mention here several reasons why.

Man had a promise of a Redeemer, and he was told that there was coming a Savior on the earth. That is the thing man should have been looking for; instead of that, he turned from God.

God had provided a sacrifice for Adam and Eve, and we find that a great, eternal principle was put down with Cain and Abel. These two boys, Cain and Abel, stand as the representatives of two great systems, two classes of people: the lost and the saved, the self-righteous and the broken-spirited, the formal professor and the genuine believer. That is what was present in the human race at this time.

And then we find that the patriarchs were living so long that the lives of Adam and Methuselah bridged the entire gap from the creation to the Flood. They certainly could have given a revelation to all mankind, which they did. Then we are told in Jude 14 and 15 that Enoch preached, he prophesied, during that period. We are also told that Noah preached during that period as he was building the ark. When Enoch disappeared, that should have alerted the people to the intervention of God in human affairs. They also knew about this man Methuselah and the meaning of his name; and when he died, they should have known the Flood was coming. Finally, there was also the ministry of the Holy Spirit. God said that His Spirit would not always strive with man. The Spirit of God *was* striving with him, but, when man totally rejected God, the Flood came in judgment upon the earth.

The entire human family has turned from God ". . . There is none righteous, no, not one" (Rom. 3:10). There are just a few, though, who do believe Him—Noah and his family. Here is one man who walked with God; he believed God. Here is a man who still trusted God—"by faith Noah." Here is a man who was willing to risk building a boat on dry land. If the rains did not come, he certainly would be the laughingstock of the community. I think he was just that for 120 years, but Noah believed God.

There is a striking comparison in the fact that the days of Noah are to be duplicated before the Lord comes again to the earth, not for the Rapture, but to establish His Kingdom. But there are some remarkable parallels that have already taken place. For instance, this chapter opened: "And it came to pass, when men began to multiply on the face of the earth, and daughters were born unto them. . . ." There was this tremendous population increase, and by that time man had spread pretty much over the earth. He was in North America, in Asia, in Europe, and in Africa. He had spread in every direction. Today we have a tremendous population explosion, and men again have increased upon the face of the earth.

Also, there is the fact that during the Great Tribulation period, the Holy Spirit will no longer restrain evil. He will be there to convert men, but we are told very definitely that He will not be restraining evil on the earth. God's overtures to men will be despised and rejected, and certainly they are even today. Isn't it amazing that the only ones who are listened to by the world today are the liberal Protestant and Roman Catholic ministers? You hear nothing from conservative men. They have attempted to make some sort of inroad, and they are trying their best to get back in the mainstream, but we have come to the day when, if you are going to stand for God, you will find that you will not be able to talk before a television camera very often. Instead, you must learn to protest, to march, and to deny Christ before you can expect a television interview!

Finally, the world in that day will be faced with the great problem of the Rapture—there will have been a great number of people who have mysteriously left the earth. Also there were judgments in Noah's day, and yet they did not heed them.

INSTRUCTIONS TO NOAH FOR BUILDING THE ARK

In the preparation for the Flood, God is giving the people ample opportunity.

> **Make thee an ark of gopher wood; rooms shalt thou make in the ark, and shalt pitch it within and without with pitch [Gen. 6:14].**

"Make thee an ark of gopher wood." Gopher wood is an almost indestructible wood very much like our redwood here in California.

"Rooms shalt thou make in the ark." The word for "rooms" has the idea of nest. The elephant would need a room, but the mole would not need quite that much space. He could be given just a little dirt in a corner, and that is all he would need.

"And shalt pitch it within and without with pitch." The ark was to be made waterproof.

> **And this is the fashion which thou shalt make it of: The length of the ark shall be three hundred cubits, the breadth of it fifty cubits, and the height of it thirty cubits [Gen. 6:15].**

The impression that most people have of the ark is the impression they were given by the little Sunday school pictures which made it look like a houseboat. It was, to me, a very ridiculous sort of a travesty. It was a caricature of the ark instead of a picture of it like it actually was.

To begin with, the instructions for the building of the ark reveal that it was quite sizable. "The length of the ark shall be three hundred cubits." If a cubit is eighteen inches, that ought to give you some conception of how long this ark was.

The question arises as to how they could make it substantial in that day. My friend, we are not dealing with cavemen. We are dealing with a very intelligent man. You see, the intelligence that the race has today came right through Noah, and he happened to be a very intelligent man.

Noah is not making an oceangoing ship to withstand fifty-foot waves. All he is building is a place for life, animal life and man, to stay over quite a period of time—not to go through a storm, but just to wait out the Flood. For that reason, the ark might lack a great deal that you would find on an oceangoing ship, and that would give it a great deal more room.

If a cubit is 18 inches, 300 cubits would mean that the ark was 450 feet long. That is a pretty long boat, but the relative measurements is the thing that interests me. For instance, I noted that the *New Mexico*, one of our battleships of the World War II era, was built 624 feet long, 106¼ feet wide, and with a mean draught of 29½ feet. By comparison the ark had practically the same ratio; so that you did not have a ridiculous looking boat at all, but one which would compare favorably with the way they build ships today.

A window shalt thou make to the ark, and in a cubit shalt thou finish it above; and the door of the ark shalt thou set in the side thereof; with lower, second, and third stories shalt thou make it [Gen. 6:16].

"A window shalt thou make to the ark." The window was not a little slit made in the side of the ark. Have you ever stopped to think about the stench that there might be with all those animals in there over that period of time? The window was a cubit high and went all the way around the top of the ark. The roof must have overlapped the window quite a bit. That is the way they ventilate a gymnasium today. I also noticed that at the state fair in Dallas, Texas, the buildings in which the animals were housed had that window which goes all the way around at the top. With all the animals they had there, it was not an unpleasant place to be. People were sitting in there eating their meals and also sleeping. It was very comfortable, and the odor was not bad. I have heard it said that poor Noah had to stick his head out this little window in order to live. That's ridiculous. That is man's imagination and not what the record says here at all.

"And the door of the ark shalt thou set in the side thereof." The ark had only one door, and that is important. Christ said, "I am the way" and "I am the door to the sheepfold," and He is the door to the ark.

"With lower, second, and third stories shalt thou make it." The ark had three decks, you see, and then, I take it, one either on top or on the bottom which would make four decks. Was there a door for each deck? I am rather of the opinion there was only one door and not one for each floor, but frankly, that is beside the point.

PASSENGERS IN THE ARK

And, behold, I, even I, do bring a flood of waters upon the earth, to destroy all flesh, wherein is the breath of life, from under heaven; and every thing that is in the earth shall die [Gen. 6:17].

God is bringing judgment upon the earth—upon animal and bird and man.

But with thee will I establish my covenant; and thou shalt come into the ark, thou, and thy sons, and thy wife, and thy sons' wives with thee.

And of every living thing of all flesh, two of every sort shalt thou bring into the ark, to keep them alive with thee; they shall be male and female.

Of fowls after their kind, and of cattle after their kind, of every creeping thing of the earth after his kind, two of every sort shall come unto thee, to keep them alive [Gen. 6:18–20].

"Two of every sort shall come unto thee, to keep them alive." Noah was not a Frank Buck who went out "to bring 'em back alive." He was not a big game hunter. He did not have to go after these animals—they came to him.

Animals in danger will do that. I remember the first time that we went into Yosemite Valley when our daughter was just a little thing. She had never seen snow before, and when we put her down in the snow, she began to whimper. But she quit when she looked over and saw a little deer. I believe we could have gone over and petted that little deer, but realizing the possible danger, of course we did not approach him any closer. When I mentioned the deer to the ranger, he laughed and said, "Yes, there's snow up in the High Sierra right now, and when there is snow up there and there's danger, they come down here and are as tame as any animal could possibly be. But the minute the snows melt in spring, they leave this area, and you couldn't get within a country mile of any of them." Why? Because when an animal is in danger, he will come to man. At the time of the Flood, I do not think Noah had any problem at all, for the animals all came to him.

And take thou unto thee of all food that is eaten, and thou shalt gather it to thee; and it shall be for food for thee, and for them.

Thus did Noah; according to all that God commanded him, so did he [Gen. 6:21–22].

Noah is now to do something very practical. It took a lot of hay in the ark to feed these animals. Some people are going to say, "But some of those animals ate meat. They would eat each other!" I do not think so. Up to the time of the Flood, apparently both men and animals were not flesh-eating. They just did not eat flesh; there were no carnivorous animals. We are told of a day in the Millennium when the lion and the lamb will lie down together, and the lion will eat straw like an ox (see Isa. 11:6–7). That could certainly come to pass, for that probably was the original state of the animal.

CHAPTER 7

THEME: Noah, his family, and the animals enter the ark; destruction of all flesh and the salvation of those in the ark

NOAH, HIS FAMILY, AND THE ANIMALS ENTER THE ARK

And the LORD said unto Noah, Come thou and all thy house into the ark; for thee have I seen righteous before me in this generation [Gen. 7:1].

Why was Noah righteous? It was by faith, just as later on Abraham was counted righteous because of his faith: "And he believed in the LORD; and he counted it to him for righteousness" (Gen. 15:6). Noah believed God, and it was counted to him for righteousness. "By faith Noah . . . prepared an ark . . ." the writer to the Hebrews said (Heb. 11:7). That is the reason God saved him.

Have you ever noticed how gracious God is to this man in all of this time of judgment? Here in verse 1 He says "Come thou. . . ." This is the same invitation that the Lord Jesus gives today to all mankind: "Come unto me, all ye that labour and are heavy laden, and I will you rest" (Matt. 11:28). Then in verse 16 of this chapter, we read, "And the LORD shut him in." Isn't that lovely? And finally, chapter 8 opens, "And God remembered Noah." How wonderful! God could very easily have forgotten all about Noah. Years later He could have said, "Oh my, I forgot all about that fellow down there. I put him in an ark and forgot about him!" That would have been too bad, wouldn't it? But God did not forget. God remembered Noah. God never forgets. He remembers you. The only thing that He does not remember is your sin if you have come to Him for salvation. Your sins He remembers no more. What a beautiful thing this is!

Now Noah and his family enter into the ark. Did you know that this story of Noah, just like the story of creation, has wandered over the face of the earth? I wish that I could give you the Babylonian account. All you have to do is to compare them to see the differences. The other accounts are utterly preposterous and ridiculous. The very fact that most nations and peoples have an account of both creation and the Flood should tell you something, my friend. It ought to tell you that there is a basis of truth for them. All of these peoples would not come up with such a record if they had been making up stories. And if you want to know which one is accurate, just make a comparison. The Babylonian account, for example, is a perfectly ridiculous story of a sort of war going on among the gods, one against the other, and that is what brought the Flood. In contrast, the Bible tells us that the Flood was a judgment of God upon man for his sin—that makes sense, by the way.

Of every clean beast thou shalt take to thee by sevens, the male and his female: and of beasts that are not clean by two, the male and his female.

Of fowls also of the air by sevens, the male and the female; to keep seed alive upon the face of all the earth [Gen. 7:2–3].

This was the basis of a lawsuit years ago against Dr. Harry Rimmer who had offered a thousand dollars to anyone who could show a contradiction in the Bible. There were several liberal theologians who testified in a court of law that this was a contradiction. Why would it first say two of each kind and now seven of each kind? Of course Dr. Rimmer won the lawsuit. All you have to do is turn over to see that when Noah got out of the ark, he offered clean beasts as sacrifices. Where would he have gotten the clean beasts if he had not taken more than two? It was only of the clean beasts that he took seven, and now we know why. Those that were not clean went in by twos, a male and a female.

"Of fowls also of the air by sevens, the male and the female"—that is for those that are clean.

> For yet seven days, and I will cause it to rain upon the earth forty days and forty nights; and every living substance that I have made will I destroy from off the face of the earth [Gen. 7:4].

For seven days the world could have knocked at the door of the ark, and frankly, they could have come in—God would have saved them. All they had to do was to believe God.

> And Noah was six hundred years old when the flood of waters was upon the earth.
>
> And Noah went in, and his sons, and his wife, and his sons' wives with him, into the ark, because of the waters of the flood.
>
> Of clean beasts, and of beasts that are not clean, and of fowls, and of every thing that creepeth upon the earth,
>
> There went in two and two unto Noah into the ark, the male and the female, as God had commanded Noah [Gen. 7:6–9].

Nowhere does Scripture say that Noah went out and drove the animals in. It was not necessary—they came to him.

DESTRUCTION OF ALL FLESH AND THE SALVATION OF THOSE IN THE ARK

> In the six hundredth year of Noah's life, in the second month, the seventeenth day of the month, the same day were all the fountains of the great deep broken up, and the windows of heaven were opened.
>
> And the rain was upon the earth forty days and forty nights.

And they that went in, went in male and female of all flesh, as God had commanded him: and the LORD shut him in.

And the flood was forty days upon the earth; and the waters increased, and bare up the ark, and it was lift up above the earth [Gen. 7:11–12, 16–17].

What is the scientific, historical evidence for the Flood? I am not going to enter into this subject other than to mention one of the finest books on this subject which I can highly recommend. It is *The Genesis Flood* by Henry M. Morris and John C. Whitcomb (Presbyterian and Reformed, 1960). Both of these men are thoroughly qualified to write on this subject. John Whitcomb, Th.D., professor of Old Testament at Grace Theological Seminary, and Henry M. Morris, Ph.D. from the University of Minnesota, professor of hydraulic engineering and chairman of the Department of Civil Engineering in the Virginia Polytechnic Institute, joined together and have written a book on the Genesis Flood. They show that the Flood was universal, it was a great catastrophe, and there is historical evidence for it. They also answer the uniformitarian argument (that existing processes acting in the same manner as at present are sufficient to account for all geological changes). This is one of the many different theories that have been advanced to discount the geological evidences of the universal Flood. I assume that there is an abundance of historical evidence for the Flood, and it is not necessary for me to go into it, as it has been answered in this very scholarly book.

And every living substance was destroyed which was upon the face of the ground, both man, and cattle, and the creeping things, and the fowl of the heaven; and they were destroyed from the earth: and Noah only remained alive, and they that were with him in the ark [Gen. 7:23].

On the other hand, there have recently come from the press several books by men whom I consider to be pseudointellectuals and pseudotheologians. They take the position that the Flood was local; that is, that it was confined to the Tigris-Euphrates Valley. In other words, it was sort of a big swimming pool and that is about all. *The Genesis Flood* absolutely demolishes that thought altogether, and I am sure that you realize that the Scriptures make it very clear that the Flood covered the whole earth. God said that the entire earth was going to be destroyed by the Flood. "And God said unto Noah, The end of all flesh is come before me; for the earth is filled with violence through them; and, behold, I will destroy them with the earth" (Gen. 6:13).

The human family had already gotten to North America, and the animals were certainly there—nobody would argue that point for a moment. But if you say that the Flood was not universal, then you have someone besides Noah starting the human family over again— and that is just not the way the Word of God tells it. You are on the horns of a dilemma, as I see it: you either have to accept the Word of God, or you have to reject what it says. To my judgment, to attempt to make a case for a local flood is actually, in the long run, to reject the Word of God. The Bible makes it very clear that it was a universal flood. "And every living substance was destroyed . . . and Noah only remained alive, and they that were with him in the ark."

And the waters prevailed upon the earth an hundred and fifty days [Gen. 7:24].

In other words, for a period of approximately half a year, for five months, the waters prevailed on the earth.

The Genesis Flood not only answers the question of its being a universal rather than a local flood, but it also answers this question of uniformitarianism. There are those who take the position that there was no such thing as a great convulsion or catastrophe like the Flood. I am not going into detail, except to point out that Peter makes it very clear that we should expect such scoffers. "Knowing this first, that there shall come in the last days scoffers, walking after their own lusts, And saying, Where is the promise of his coming? for since the fathers fell asleep, all things continue as they were from the beginning of the creation" (2 Pet. 3:3–4). The scoffer has always been a uniformitarian, but you could not very well hold that position and accept the integrity of the Word of God at this particular point. This is very important to see.

CHAPTER 8

THEME: The rains cease; earth dries—Noah leaves the ark; Noah builds an altar and offers sacrifice

THE RAINS CEASE

And God remembered Noah, and every living thing, and all the cattle that was with him in the ark: and God made a wind to pass over the earth, and the waters assuaged;

The fountains also of the deep and the windows of heaven were stopped, and the rain from heaven was restrained;

And the waters returned from off the earth continually: and after the end of the hundred and fifty days the waters were abated.

And the ark rested in the seventh month, on the seventeenth day of the month, upon the mountains of Ararat [Gen. 8:1–4].

We are given the record not only of the building up of the Flood but also of the prevailing and now the assuaging of the Flood. We are told that "God remembered Noah"—how lovely—and that "God made a wind to pass over the earth, and the waters assuaged." It did not happen just overnight. The buildup of the waters took over 150 days, and then there were 261 days in the assuaging. That looks to me like it is something more than just a local flood.

And the waters decreased continually until the tenth month: in the tenth month, on the first day of the month, were the tops of the mountains seen.

> And it came to pass at the end of forty days, that Noah
> opened the window of the ark which he had made [Gen.
> 8:5-6].

We could say that this is the beginning of the end of the Flood. Notice
what Noah does:

> And he sent forth a raven, which went forth to and fro,
> until the waters were dried up from off the earth.

> Also he sent forth a dove from him, to see if the waters
> were abated from off the face of the ground [Gen. 8:7-8].

Frankly, Noah becomes a bird-watcher. He sends out these two birds,
the raven and the dove.

> But the dove found no rest for the sole of her foot, and
> she returned unto him into the ark, for the waters were
> on the face of the whole earth: then he put forth his
> hand, and took her, and pulled her in unto him into the
> ark.

> And he stayed yet other seven days; and again he sent
> forth the dove out of the ark;

> And the dove came in to him in the evening; and, lo, in
> her mouth was an olive leaf plucked off: so Noah knew
> that the waters were abated from off the earth.

> And he stayed yet other seven days; and sent forth the
> dove; which returned not again unto him any more
> [Gen. 8:9-12].

I want you to see a great spiritual truth that we have here in the eighth
chapter in this account of the raven and the dove. After Noah had
spent over a year in the ark, he sent forth a raven, and the raven never
came back. But the dove kept coming back and even brought in its

beak a little bit of greenery, an olive leaf. I do not know why the dove and olive leaf have always been symbolic of peace, but they are. I cannot quite see that that is exactly the message of the dove's second return. But when the dove did not return at all, that was the sign that the judgment was over and that peace had returned to the earth. But, of course, man going out of the ark is the same type of man that all the sons of Adam were who had provoked the Flood as a judgment from God in the first place. You are going to see that there is not too much improvement in man after the Flood; in fact, there is none whatsoever.

There is a great spiritual lesson here which I would not have you miss for anything in the world. Noah is engaged here in "bird-watching." He sends out the raven, and the raven does not come back. Why didn't that raven come back? You must recognize what that raven eats—it feeds on carrion. There was a whole lot of flesh of dead animals floating around after the Flood, and that was the kind of thing this old crow ate. He did not return to the ark because he was really going to a feast, and he was having a very wonderful time. The raven was classified as an unclean bird, by the way.

The dove is a clean bird and is so listed later on in Scripture. Remember that Noah took into the ark both the clean and the unclean animals. The dove brought back information: it was a regular homing pigeon. With the dove's second trip, Noah was now a confirmed bird-watcher—and the dove brought back evidence that the dry land was appearing. The third time, the dove did not return, and Noah knew that the waters of judgment were gone.

I have said before that all great truths of the Bible are germane in Genesis. The Bible teaches that the believer has two natures, an old and a new nature: "Therefore if any man be in Christ, he is a new creature: old things are passed away; behold, all things are become new" (2 Cor. 5:17).

The clean and the unclean are together. You and I as believers have these two natures. Our Lord said: "That which is born of the flesh is flesh; and that which is born of the Spirit is spirit" (John 3:6). And Paul writes: "For I know that in me (that is, in my flesh,) dwelleth no good thing: for to will is present with me; but how to perform that which is good I find not" (Rom. 7:18).

Paul spoke of a struggle between the two natures. And there is a struggle today between the old nature and the new nature of a believer.

The raven went out into a judged world, but he found a feast in the dead carcass because that is the thing he lived on. The bloated carcass of an elephant would have made him a banquet; I tell you, it would have been for him a bacchanalian orgy. Back and forth, he restlessly went up and down. May I say to you, that is the picture of the old nature; the old nature is like that raven. The old nature loves the things of the world and feasts on them. That is the reason so many people watch television on Sunday night and do not go to church. Don't tell me that you have some good excuse for that. You do have an old nature, but that is no excuse because you ought not to be living in the old nature.

The dove went out into a judged world, but she found no rest, no satisfaction, and she returned to the ark. The dove represents the believer in the world. The old raven went out into the world and loved it. When he found that old carcass, he probably thought the Millennium had arrived! You see, it is a matter of viewpoint. A professor said to me, "This matter of what's right and wrong is relative." He's right; it is. It is what God says is right, and it is what the professor says is wrong—and he does not find very much that is wrong, by the way. What God says is wrong *is* wrong. The believer is told, "Love not the world, neither the things that are in the world . . ." (1 John 2:15). You and I are living in a judged world today. We are in the world, but not of it. We are to use it, but not abuse it. We are not to fall in love with it, but we are to attempt to win the lost in this world and get out the Word of God. Our Lord told us, ". . . Go ye into all the world, and preach the gospel to every creature" (Mark 16:15). Let's take care of our job down here and get out the Word of God—that is the important thing. The dove recognized what kind of a world she was in, and she found no rest. She found rest only in the ark, and that ark sets forth Christ, if you please.

Let me ask you this very personal question: What kind of bird are you? Are you a raven or a dove? If you are a child of God, you have both natures—but which one are you living in today? Do you love the things of God, or don't you?

EARTH DRIES—NOAH LEAVES THE ARK

And it came to pass in the six hundredth and first year, in the first month, the first day of the month, the waters were dried up from off the earth: and Noah removed the covering of the ark, and looked, and, behold, the face of the ground was dry [Gen. 8:13].

This brings us to 261 days, so that the total time of the Flood was 371 days, extending over a year. That also conforms to the statement of Scripture that the Flood was universal; it was not just the filling of a swimming pool—it certainly was more than that!

There have been other discoveries that have revealed something concerning the Flood, and I would like to pass on to you the words of Dr. J. E. Shelley who takes the position that the Flood was universal, that it covered the entire earth: "The most striking example of this is found in the case of the mammoths. These elephants are found buried in the frozen silt of the Tundra, Siberia, all over the length of the Continent of Asia, and in the North of Alaska and Canada. They are found in herds on the higher ground not bogged in marshes, hundreds of thousands in number." He goes on to say that these elephants have been examined and found to have drowned. If they had just gotten bogged down, they would have died of starvation.

"The farther north one goes, the more there are, till the soil of the islands of the White Sea inside the Arctic circle consists largely of their bones mingled with those of sabre-tooth tiger, giant elk, cave bear, musk ox, and with trunks of trees and trees rooted in the soil. There are now no trees in those regions, the nearest being hundreds almost thousands of miles away. The mammoth could not eat the stunted vegetation which now grows in this region for but three months in the year, a hundred square miles of which would not keep one of them alive for a month. The food in their stomachs is pine, hawthorn branches, etc. These mammoths were buried alive in the silt when that silt was soft. They and the silt were then suddenly frozen and have never been unfrozen. For they show no signs of decomposition. Mammoth ivory has been sold on the London docks for more than a thousand years. The Natural History Museum purchased a mammoth's head and tusks from the ivory store of the London Docks. This head was absolutely fresh and was covered with its original fur."

If you doubt the universality of the Flood, here is more than enough evidence to convince you.

And Noah went forth, and his sons, and his wife, and his sons' wives with him:

Every beast, every creeping thing, and every fowl, and whatsoever creepeth upon the earth, after their kinds, went forth out of the ark [Gen. 8:18-19].

NOAH BUILDS AN ALTAR AND OFFERS SACRIFICE

God is now going to make a covenant with Noah. We will see this new beginning as we get into the next chapter. This covenant is a very important one. When God made it with Noah, He made it with the human family that is on the earth today.

And Noah builded an altar unto the LORD; and took of every clean beast, and of every clean fowl, and offered burnt offerings on the altar [Gen. 8:20].

Now do you see why Noah took seven of the clean beasts and only two of the unclean? He is now offering the clean beasts as sacrifices.

The first thing that Noah did when he came out of the ark was to build an altar to the Lord and offer a sacrifice, a burnt offering, to Him. That burnt offering speaks of the person of Jesus Christ. It was offered on the basis of acceptance before God and of praise to God in recognition of Him. Without doubt, this was one of the things that caused God to be pleased with Noah at this particular time.

> And the LORD smelled a sweet savour; and the LORD said
> in his heart, I will not again curse the ground any more
> for man's sake; for the imagination of man's heart is evil
> from his youth; neither will I again smite any more
> every thing living, as I have done [Gen. 8:21].

You can just write it down that that is true. What about your youth?
Was your imagination evil or not? In our contemporary society we can
see the rebellion of youth, and isn't it interesting to note the direction
they have gone? They have gone in the same direction. Every imagination of man's heart is evil from his youth—and it does not improve. I
was visiting in a hospital the other night. The curtain was pulled between the beds, but you could hear the next patient talking with her
husband. It seemed to be a contest between those two to see who
could outcuss the other one! I have never heard such profanity on the
part of two human beings. May I say to you, the imagination of man's
heart is evil from his youth. That just happens to be an accurate statement that was made a long time ago.

> While the earth remaineth, seedtime and harvest, and
> cold and heat, and summer and winter, and day and
> night shall not cease [Gen. 8:22].

It has been suggested that the Flood was so extensive that it tilted the
earth. As you know, the earth is not straight on its axis. We are off
center, if you please. The magnetic center is different from the center
on which we are revolving. Something happened somewhere along
the line, and it is the belief of many that this is when it took place.
Because the earth revolves like that, that gives us our seasons. It is sort
of going around like a wobbly top. You remember that when you were
young and would spin a top, the top would run down and get wobbly.
That is the way the earth revolves today, and as a result we have the
seasons.
    Prior to the Flood, man learned the three R's: (1) *Rebellion* against
God was *realized*—it came right out in the open. (2) *Revelation* from
God was *rejected* by man. Noah's witness did not reach them.

(3) *Repentance* was absolutely *repudiated*; there was no return to God at all. Men refused the refuge that God provided, and for 120 years Noah had no converts. These are the three R's. Men led in rebellion, they rejected the revelation, and there was no repentance on their part.

Now as this man Noah comes forth from the ark, he stands in a most unique position. He stands in the position of being the head of the human race again—the same position Adam had. It is said that we are all related to Adam, but we are closer kin than that: we are all related in Noah. In one sense, Noah is the father of all of us today.

1-14-'08 Monday

Noah didn't reach man in those days of building the ARK - & must keep "building" regardless of The rebellion around me.

CHAPTER 9

THEME: New instructions and arrangements; the sin of
Noah and his sons

Now we come to a new beginning. It is difficult for us to realize
what a revolutionary beginning it is. The dispensation of human
conscience is over, and God is putting man under government—he is
to govern himself. We will see something of this in the covenant
which God made with Noah. And let's keep in mind that, when God
made the covenant with Noah, He made it with you and me, for He
made it with all mankind.

NEW INSTRUCTIONS AND ARRANGEMENTS

**And God blessed Noah and his sons, and said unto
them, Be fruitful, and multiply, and replenish the earth
[Gen. 9:1].**

The word *replenish* is meaningful here because we know that there
was a civilization before the Flood, and now there is to be a civilization after the Flood. (When Adam was told to replenish the earth, we
assume that there had been living creatures—I don't know what to
call them—before Adam. They apparently were living creatures of
God's creation; anything I could say beyond that would be pure speculation.)

Notice that the first thing God tells Noah to do is to "be fruitful,
and multiply, and replenish the earth." There is to be the propagation
of the race. Remember that God gave this command under special cir-
cumstances. Today we are in a time of population explosion, and
there is overpopulation that is quite dangerous. However, Noah stood
in a unique position. He and his family were the only folk around.
Can you imagine driving down the freeway, going to work in the
morning, and there are cars in front of you, cars to the right of you,

cars to the left of you, cars behind you, cars honking—you're in a traffic snarl. Then about a year later you go out on the freeway and there is not another car there. Yours is the only one. You might as well take down all the traffic lights. You won't need them because you are the only one driving through. This would be quite an unusual experience for us, would it not? Well, this was the experience of Noah in his day.

> **And the fear of you and the dread of you shall be upon every beast of the earth, and upon every fowl of the air, upon all that moveth upon the earth, and upon all the fishes of the sea; into your hand are they delivered [Gen. 9:2].**

Another part of the covenant is man's protection and rulership over the animal world. I take it that before this time the relationship was different. Apparently man had not been a meat eater before. All the animals were tame, and one is not inclined to eat an animal that is a pet. Remember that the animals *came* to Noah when the Flood was impending; they seemed to have no fear of him at all.

Now the animals will fear and dread man. However, man is responsible for the animal world. Man's treatment of the animal world is a brutal story. Man has attempted to exterminate many of the animals. Man would have slaughtered all the whales around the Hawaiian Islands for the money they could get if the government had not intervened. At one time the buffalo were in great herds in the West, but they were killed by man. Today we must have places of refuge to protect animals and bird life. It is well that we do that. The animals of Africa are being exterminated. Man is a mighty brutal creature. We need a government to protect the animals from man.

> **Every moving thing that liveth shall be meat for you; even as the green herb have I given you all things [Gen. 9:3].**

Now God gives to man a new provision for food. Before the Flood God gave to man the green earth, the plant life, to eat. Now He tells Noah that he is able to eat animal life. There are diet faddists, and often this type of thing becomes a part of a person's religion. I once met a lady who was a vegetarian as a part of her religion, and she was quite excited when I told her that these antediluvians were all vegetarians. She thought this reinforced her argument that we should all be vegetarians, and she had her assistant take it down in her notes. However, I think she must have erased it later because I told her this: "I wouldn't make too much of it if I were you because you must remember that it was a bunch of vegetarians who were destroyed in the Flood. If diet had in any way improved them at that time, they would not have been destroyed." We see here that God now permits man to eat flesh.

However, God prohibits the eating of blood.

But flesh with the life thereof, which is the blood thereof, shall ye not eat [Gen. 9:4].

The blood should be drained out. The blood speaks of life; draining it indicates that the animal should be killed in a merciful way rather than prolonging its suffering and that it must be really dead. Although I enjoy the sport of hunting, I don't like to shoot quail, for instance, because sometimes I just wound the little fellow and it crawls away so that I can't find it. I don't like to do that. God says that when you are going to eat animals, you are to make sure that you don't eat them with their blood. It should be drained out, ensuring that the animal is killed in a merciful manner.

And surely your blood of your lives will I require; at the hand of every beast will I require it, and at the hand of man; at the hand of every man's brother will I require the life of man [Gen. 9:5].

This is an interesting statement, but not so meaningful to those of us who do not live on a frontier. However, there are certain animals even we encounter—such as skunks and opossums which may be rabid or disease-carrying rodents—that pose a real danger to man.

Now the fifth and the last statement in the new covenant is the most amazing—

Whoso sheddeth man's blood, by man shall his blood be shed: for in the image of God made he man [Gen. 9:6].

Here God lays down the principle for government and protection of man. He gives the government the right of capital punishment. We have seen that in this new covenant which God has given, man is to propagate the race, he is to have the protectorate and the rulership over animals, he is given a new provision for food and a prohibition against the eating of blood. Now we see that he is given the principle of government, which is the basis of capital punishment.

May I say to you that it is amazing how the attitude of the present generation has gotten away from the Bible. You see, we do not have a Bible-oriented population anymore. It is almost totally ignorant of the Word of God. As a result, we find the judges, the lawyers, and the politicians all wanting to get rid of capital punishment. They have succeeded in many cases, and I think that finally it will be eliminated totally from American culture. At the same time we have an increase in crime and the most horrible crimes taking place. I have dealt with this subject more in detail in a booklet which I entitled, *Is Capital Punishment Christian?* I believe that capital punishment is scriptural and that it is the basis of government. The government has the right to take a life when that individual has taken someone else's life. Why? Well, I think it is quite obvious that God has ruled it so in order to protect human life.

Our lives are no longer safe on the streets and often not in our homes, either. Although I know that many officials would deny this, one reason is our attitude toward capital punishment. When a criminal knows that if he takes a life, his life is going to be sacrificed, then may I say to you, he'll think twice before he takes a life. Also, there is an idea today about getting a gun-control law. May I say that the problem is not with the gun in the hand, it is with the heart inside the man.

"Whoso sheddeth man's blood, by man shall his blood be shed" is

a law that we had better get back on our statute books and get rid of
this sob-sister stuff. Human government is the area into which all
mankind has moved (Gentiles included). "Whoso sheddeth man's
blood, by man shall his blood be shed: for in the image of God made
he man" is the basis for human government. It has not been changed
as far as the governments of the world are concerned.

> **And you, be ye fruitful, and multiply; bring forth abun-
> dantly in the earth, and multiply therein [Gen. 9:7].**

This is a repetition of God's instructions in verse 1.

> **And God spake unto Noah, and to his sons with him,
> saying,**
>
> **And I, behold, I establish my covenant with you, and
> with your seed after you [Gen. 9:8–9].**

"With your seed after you" includes all the human race.

> **And with every living creature that is with you, of the
> fowl, of the cattle, and of every beast of the earth with
> you; from all that go out of the ark, to every beast of the
> earth [Gen. 9:10].**

All of God's creatures are included in this covenant. Isaiah predicts
that someday the lion and the lamb will lie down together and that
they will not hurt or destroy each other. In Paul's Epistle to the Romans he mentions that the whole creation is groaning and travailing
in pain in this present age. May I say to you that God has made this
covenant with Noah and with all of His creatures until the time His
Kingdom comes on earth. It is for all of Noah's descendants and
"every living creature that is with you."

> **And I will establish my covenant with you; neither shall
> all flesh be cut off any more by the waters of a flood;**

> **neither shall there any more be a flood to destroy the earth [Gen. 9:11].**

This is God's promise. His purpose is that He will not again destroy the earth with a flood. The next time His judgment of the earth will be by fire. We find that stated in 2 Peter 3.

In the next few verses we see the picture of the covenant, and in my opinion, really a spiritual meaning of the covenant. It is sort of a sacrament, if you please. The thing which makes it that is a visible sign to which are annexed promises.

> **And God said, This is the token of the covenant which I make between me and you and every living creature that is with you, for perpetual generations:**
>
> **I do set my bow in the cloud, and it shall be for a token of a covenant between me and the earth [Gen. 9:12–13].**

The rainbow is more or less of a sacrament, that is, a token of a covenant.

> **And it shall come to pass, when I bring a cloud over the earth, that the bow shall be seen in the cloud:**
>
> **And I will remember my covenant, which is between me and you and every living creature of all flesh; and the waters shall no more become a flood to destroy all flesh.**
>
> **And the bow shall be in the cloud; and I will look upon it, that I may remember the everlasting covenant between God and every living creature of all flesh that is upon the earth [Gen. 9:14–16].**

Notice that God says, "I will look upon it" and "I will remember." God didn't say that you would see it; He said that He would see it. He said He would look upon it and it would be an "everlasting covenant between God and every living creature of all flesh that is upon the earth." That ought to be the encouragement whenever you look at a rainbow.

And God said unto Noah, This is the token of the covenant, which I have established between me and all flesh that is upon the earth [Gen. 9:17].

This is God's covenant, not merely with Noah but with all flesh that is upon the earth.

Let me say again that the rainbow could be called a sacrament because a sacrament is a visible sign to which are annexed certain promises. The Passover feast, the brazen serpent, Gideon's fleece, and in our day, baptism and the Lord's Supper are such signs.

Dr. Johann Peter Lange once made the statement, "God's eye of grace and our eye of faith meet in the sacraments." That is what happens when man looks at the rainbow. Faith lays hold of the promise attached to the sign. You see, the merit is in what the sign speaks of. There is no faith in a promise and there is no assurance in a sign—the word and the sign go together, you see. God makes a promise and attaches a sign to it. Now the rainbow is God's answer to Noah's altar. It is as if God says, "I'll remember, and I'll look upon it." A friend of mine told me about a time he was traveling by plane across the country and going over a storm. The plane was up where the sun was shining, and all of a sudden he saw a rainbow that went all the way around, a complete circle. I guess that is the way God always sees it.

THE SIN OF NOAH AND HIS SONS

We will find something that is very disappointing in the remainder of this chapter. The question arises: When man came out of the ark after the Flood and all the sinners were dead, does that mean that there was no more sin on the earth? Well, let's look and see.

And the sons of Noah, that went forth of the ark, were Shem, and Ham, and Japheth: and Ham is the father of Canaan [Gen. 9:18].

Why is Ham's son Canaan mentioned here? For two reasons. One reason we'll see in a moment. Another reason is that when Moses wrote this record, the people of Israel were traveling to the land of Canaan, and it was encouraging for them to have this information regarding God's judgment upon the people of Canaan.

> **These are the three sons of Noah: and of them was the whole earth overspread.**
>
> **And Noah began to be an husbandman, and he planted a vineyard:**
>
> **And he drank of the wine, and was drunken; and he was uncovered within his tent [Gen. 9:19–21].**

Here is the record of Noah's sin. The hard fact of the matter is that Noah got drunk, and this is sin. There is no satisfactory excuse, although many expositors have attempted to find excuses for him. One excuse is that he was ignorant of the effect of wine since no one had been drunk before. You will notice that before the Flood, drunkenness is not mentioned as one of the sins. Then there are those who hold the canopy theory about the Flood. (There are many things I have not had time to mention.) The canopy theory is that before the Flood there was an ice covering which the sunlight filtered through so that grapes did not ferment before the time of the Flood and that this was something new to Noah. Well, all I can say is that this is a new beginning in a new world, but it is old sin that is still there. This incident reveals this, and it was given to answer a big question, as we shall see.

> **And Ham, the father of Canaan, saw the nakedness of his father, and told his two brethren without.**
>
> **And Shem and Japheth took a garment, and laid it upon both their shoulders, and went backward, and covered the nakedness of their father; and their faces were backward, and they saw not their father's nakedness.**

And Noah awoke from his wine, and knew what his younger son had done unto him [Gen. 9:22–24].

Now notice what God says through Noah, which became part of the Noahic covenant.

And he said, Cursed be Canaan; a servant of servants shall he be unto his brethren [Gen. 9:25].

I would have you note that God said, "Cursed be *Canaan*"—He does not put a curse on *Ham*. A question that keeps arising is this: Is the curse of Ham upon the dark races? It certainly is not. To think otherwise is absolutely absurd. The Scripture does not teach it. The coloration of the skin, the pigment that is in the epidermis of the human family, is there because of sunlight from the outside not because of sin from within. There is no curse placed upon Ham; the curse was upon Canaan his son. We do not know in what way Canaan was involved in this incident. We are given only the bare record here, but we recognize that Canaan is mentioned for a very definite purpose. Let me repeat that it hasn't anything to do with color—it is not a curse of color put on a part of the human race. That teaching has been one of the sad things said about the black man. It is not fair to the black man and it is not fair to God—because He didn't say it. After all, the first two great civilizations were Hamitic—both the Babylonian and Egyptian civilizations were Hamitic.

Another question arises: Why did God give us a record of the sin of Noah? Well, if man had written the Book of Genesis, he would have done one of two things. He either would have covered up the sin of Noah by not mentioning it at all to make Noah a hero; or else he would have made Noah's sin a great deal more sordid than it was. But God recorded it for His own purposes.

First of all, as I have indicated, it was to encourage the children of Israel in entering the land of Canaan during the time of Moses and Joshua. It let them know that God had pronounced a curse upon Canaan. He had pronounced His judgment upon the race. All you have to do is read the rest of the Old Testament and secular history to discover the fulfillment of this judgment. The Canaanites have pretty much disappeared.

God had a further reason for recording the incident of Noah's sin. In Romans 15:4 we read these words: "For whatsoever things were written aforetime were written for our learning, that we through patience and comfort of the scriptures might have hope." It was recorded to let you and me know something of the weakness of the flesh. The Lord Jesus said that the spirit is willing but the flesh is weak. And in Galatians 2:16 it is made very clear that no flesh would be justified by keeping the law: ". . . for by the works of the law shall no flesh be justified." So God has given us here the story of a man who fell, revealing the weakness of the flesh.

There is no use trying to make excuses for Noah. The bare fact is that Noah got drunk.

Now, maybe you as a Christian do not get drunk. But, may I say, you and I may be living in the flesh to the extent we're just as displeasing to God as Noah was. We have, I think, a wrong conception of life in this universe that we are in. For instance, our nation has spent billions of dollars to put men on the moon, and it looks like it's not a good place to live anyway. But we spend relatively little on how to live on this earth. But God is concerned about training you and me how to live on this earth.

Let us not make some of the mistakes that are made in the consideration of this incident. We need to make it very clear that Noah did not lose his salvation. I trust that you understand that. It was an awful thing that he did—there is no excuse for it. It was his weakness of the flesh, but he was still a saved man.

And he said, Blessed be the LORD God of Shem; and Canaan shall be his servant.

God shall enlarge Japheth, and he shall dwell in the tents of Shem; and Canaan shall be his servant [Gen. 9:26–27].

As I have mentioned before, when Moses was given this revelation from God, he was leading the people of Israel to the land of Canaan. The Israelites were descendants of Shem.

And Noah lived after the flood three hundred and fifty years.

And all the days of Noah were nine hundred and fifty years: and he died [Gen. 9:28–29].

CHAPTER 10

THEME: Sons of Japheth; sons of Ham; sons of Shem

This is a chapter of genealogies, of families, which are the origin of the nations of the world. This chapter is far more important than the space I'm giving to it would indicate. If you are interested in ethnology and anthropology and the story of mankind on the earth, you may want a far deeper study than you will find here. H. S. Miller, who has his master's degree in ethnology, has charted the origin of the nations, using Genesis 10 as a basis for the threefold division of the human family, which is revealed in these three sons of Noah: Ham, Shem, and Japheth. Ethnology makes it evident, by the way, that neither the sons of Japheth nor the sons of Ham ever comprised what some folk call the lost ten tribes of Israel.

Here in chapter 10 we have the genealogies of all three sons of Noah.

> **Now these are the generations of the sons of Noah, Shem, Ham, and Japheth: and unto them were sons born after the flood [Gen. 10:1].**

First we see the genealogy of Japheth (vv. 2–5), then the genealogy of Ham (vv. 6–20)—this was the outstanding people at the very beginning—and finally the genealogy of Shem (vv. 21–32). Notice that throughout the Bible God follows this same pattern of giving the rejected line first and saying a word about it, then He drops that subject entirely and does not bring it up again. Finally, He gives the accepted line, the line which is leading to the Lord Jesus Christ.

SONS OF JAPHETH

> **The sons of Japheth; Gomer, and Magog, and Madai, and Javan, and Tubal, and Meshech, and Tiras [Gen. 10:2].**

According to H. S. Miller's chart, the Scythians, the Slavs, Russians, Bulgarians, Bohemians, Poles, Slovaks, Croatians came from Magog. The Indians and the Iranic races—Medes, Persians, Afghans, Kurds— all came from Madai. From Javan we have the Greeks, Romans, and the Romance nationalities such as French, Spanish, Portuguese, Italian, etc. Coming from Tiras are the Thracians, the Teutons, the Germans, and then from that we have the east Germanic and the European races, the north Germanic or the Scandinavians and the west Germanic, from which come the High German and the Low German, and then the Angles and the Saxons and the Jutes, the Anglo-Saxon race, the English people.

Well, I simply can't go into the whole chart, but it is an interesting study. You can see that the majority of us in America descended from these lines.

SONS OF HAM

And the sons of Ham; Cush, and Mizraim, and Phut, and Canaan [Gen. 10:6].

As you can see, Ham had other sons, but the curse was only upon Canaan. Why it was not upon the others, I am not prepared to say. From Canaan came the Phoenicians, the Hittites, the Jebusites, the Amorites, the Girgashites, the Hivites, etc.

From Ham's son Cush came the Africans—the Ethopians, the Egyptians, the Libyans, etc. All of these races are Hamitic, you see. Now we have some detail regarding a son of Cush—

And Cush begat Nimrod: he began to be a mighty one in the earth.

He was a mighty hunter before the Lord: wherefore it is said, Even as Nimrod the mighty hunter before the Lord [Gen. 10:8–9].

"He began to be a mighty one in the earth." He wanted to become the ruler of a great world empire, and he attempted to do it.

"He was a mighty hunter before the LORD." This doesn't mean that he was a wild game hunter. Sometimes a little boy is given an air gun, and when he goes out and shoots a sparrow, his folks say, "My, look at that! He's a little Nimrod. He hit a sparrow!" But Nimrod wasn't shooting sparrows or hunting wild game in Africa. He was a hunter of men's souls—that is the thought in this passage.

And the beginning of his kingdom was Babel, and Erech, and Accad, and Calneh, in the land of Shinar [Gen. 10:10].

He was the founder of those great cities in the land of Shinar.

Nimrod has quite a story which you can get from secular history. Alexander Hislop, in his book, *The Two Babylons*, gives the background which I am not going to repeat here, but it is a fascinating story of how Nimrod was responsible for the Tower of Babel. It was he who attempted to bring together the human race after the Flood in an effort to get them united into a nation of which he could become the great world ruler. He was the rebel, the founder of Babel, the hunter of the souls of men. He was the lawless one, and he is a shadow or a type of the last world ruler, the Antichrist who is yet to appear.

The first great civilization, therefore, came out from the sons of Ham. We need to recognize that. It is so easy today to fall into the old patterns that we were taught in school a few years ago. Now the black man is wanting more study of his race. I don't blame him. He hasn't been given an opportunity in the past several hundred years. The story of the beginning of the black man is that he headed up the first two great civilizations that appeared on this earth. They were from the sons of Ham. Nimrod was a son of Ham.

I'm not going to attempt to develop that line any further. You see, we are following the pattern set by the Holy Spirit in which He gives the rejected line first and then drops it. We are going to turn now to the line that will lead to Abraham and then to the nation Israel and finally to the coming of Christ into this world. It is this line which we will follow through the Old Testament. God is bidding good-bye to the rest of humanity for the time being, but He will be coming back to them later on.

Let me give you a quotation from Saphir's book, *The Divine Unity of Scripture:*

> The tenth chapter of Genesis is a very remarkable chapter. Before God leaves, as it were, the nations to themselves and begins to deal with Israel, His chosen people from Abraham downward, He takes a loving farewell of all the nations of the earth, as much as to say, "I am going to leave you for a while, but I love you. I have created you: I have ordered all your future; and their different genealogies are traced."

In chapter 10 seventy nations are listed. Fourteen of them are from Japheth. Thirty of them come from Ham. Don't forget that. It will give you a different conception of the black man at his beginning. And twenty-six nations come from Shem, making a total of seventy nations listed in this genealogy.

It seems to me that God is showing us what He has done with the nations of the world. Why has the white man in our day been so prominent? Well, I'll tell you why. Because at the beginning it was the black man, the colored races, that were prominent. Then the sons of Shem made a tremendous impact upon this world during the time of David and Solomon. And you will notice that from Shem there came others, such as the Syrians, the Lydians, and the Armenians, also the Arabians from Joktan. These great nations appeared next. Apparently we are currently in the period in which the white man has come to the front. It seems to me that all three are demonstrating that, regardless of whether they are a son of Ham or a son of Shem or a son of Japheth, they are incapable of ruling this world. I believe that God is demonstrating this to us, and to see this is a tremendous thing.

SONS OF SHEM

Unto Shem also, the father of all the children of Eber, the brother of Japheth the elder, even to him were children born [Gen. 10:21].

And unto Eber were born two sons: the name of one was Peleg; for in his days was the earth divided; and his brother's name was Joktan [Gen. 10:25].

When I went over this verse in a previous Bible study, I received all sorts of weird interpretations of what was meant by "the earth was divided"—that it refers to a physical division here in the earth, that the earth had undergone some tremendous physical catastrophe. Well, my friend, all that Moses is simply doing is anticipating the next chapter in which he will give us the account of the Tower of Babel. At *that* time the earth was divided. May I say that the simple interpretation seems to be the one that a great many folk miss, and we should not miss it.

Now let's just pick up the final verse of this chapter—

These are the families of the sons of Noah, after their generations, in their nations: and by these were the nations divided in the earth after the flood [Gen. 10:32].

I want to submit to you that this is one of the great chapters of the Bible although we have given very little space to it. You can see what a rich study this would make for anyone who really wanted a fair appraisal of the human family. A great many have used this remarkable chapter for that purpose.

CHAPTER 11

THEME: The building of the Tower of Babel; from Shem to Abraham

THE BUILDING OF THE TOWER OF BABEL

And the whole earth was of one language, and of one speech [Gen. 11:1].

I do not know what language the people spoke at that time. A friend of mine who was a fellow Texan, a preacher in Texas, facetiously said to me, "You and I are probably the only two who really know what they spoke before the Tower of Babel because it was Texan." Well, I'll be honest with you, I've come to the conclusion that it could have been something else. What the language was, we simply do not know. I believe whatever that language was will be the language that will be spoken in heaven, and it will be a much better language than we have today, with more specific nouns and verbs, adverbs, and adjectives.

And it came to pass, as they journeyed from the east, that they found a plain in the land of Shinar; and they dwelt there [Gen. 11:2].

"As they journeyed from the east"—notice it was *from* the east. Mankind was apparently moving toward the west. "They found a plain in the land of Shinar," which is in the Tigris-Euphrates Valley.

And they said one to another, Go to, let us make brick, and burn them thoroughly. And they had brick for stone, and slime had they for mortar [Gen. 11:3].

Down in that area there is no stone, and so they made bricks. That in itself reveals something about the substantial character of their buildings. Even today brick is a popular type of building material. Yet the brick was used there because of its practicality; it was a necessity.

And they said, Go to, let us build us a city and a tower, whose top may reach unto heaven; and let us make us a name, lest we be scattered abroad upon the face of the whole earth [Gen. 11:4].

Notice that they said, "Let us build us a city . . . and let us make us a name, lest we be scattered abroad." They had a bad case of perpendicular I-itis—let us make us a name! In my opinion, the sole purpose of this tower was for a rallying place for man.

The Tower of Babel was a ziggurat. There are many ruins of ziggurats in the Tigris-Euphrates Valley. I have a picture of the ruins of one in Ur of the Chaldees where Abraham lived. It was made of brick, solidly constructed, and around it was a runway which went to the top. Apparently, on top of it was an altar on which, in certain instances, human sacrifices were offered. Later on children were offered, put in a red-hot idol. All of this was connected with the ziggurat in later history.

But at the time of its construction, the Tower of Babel represented the rebellion of mankind against Almighty God. Apparently it was Nimrod who led in this movement. He was the builder of the city of Babel and evidently of the Tower of Babel also. It was to be a place for him to rear a world empire that was in opposition to God.

In order to realize his ambition and to make his dreams come true, two features and factors were essential: First, he needed a center of unity, a sort of headquarters, as it were. He needed a capital, a place to assemble, a place to look to. This was why he built the city of Babel. It fulfilled one of his requirements to carry out his dream of world empire. Secondly, he needed a rallying point, not just geographical but psychological, that which gives motive—a spark, an inspiration, a song, a battle cry, sort of like a "rally-around-the-flag-boys." There had to be some impelling and compelling motivation. There had to be a monument, Lenin's tomb is where Communism meets, and in Nimrod's day it was the Tower of Babel. "Let us make us" is defiance and rebellion against God. "Let us make us a *name*" reveals an overweening ambition.

Now let's see what the Tower of Babel was *not*. It was not built as a place of refuge in time of high water. He wasn't building above the flood stage, as some expositors suggest. In fact, I consider that a very puerile interpretation. After all, Lenin's tomb is not a place of refuge when the Volga River overflows! No, this tower revealed the arrogant, defiant, rebellious attitude of man against God. God had said to man that he should scatter over the earth and replenish the earth. But man in essence answered, "Nothing doing. We're not going to scatter; we are going to get together. We are through with You." The Tower of Babel was against God.

Also, the Tower of Babel was a religious symbol. It was a ziggurat. All through that valley, as I have indicated, there are ruins of ziggurats. They were places where people worshiped the creature rather than the Creator. Some ziggurats were round, others were square, but all of them had runways leading to the top, and on the top the people carried on the worship of the sun, moon, and stars. After all, when they could see the sun, moon, and stars, they knew they were not going to have a flood, and they felt that God had been pretty mean to have sent the Flood.

Now notice God's reaction to the Tower of Babel—

And the Lord came down to see the city and the tower, which the children of men builded.

And the Lord said, Behold, the people is one, and they have all one language; and this they begin to do: and now nothing will be restrained from them, which they have imagined to do [Gen. 11:5–6].

This is a tremendous statement! Since all the people spoke one language, they didn't have the great language barrier. They could get together and pool their knowledge and resources—"and now nothing will be restrained from them, which they have imagined to do." We find here that man has a fallen nature in spite of the Flood and that he is totally depraved. God cannot ignore this rebellion, for it is a rebellion against Him. God is going to put up a protective wall. He is going to throw up a barrier. This was necessary because man is such a very capable creature. He can go to the moon and he can fly in a jet plane. I still am amazed that I can sit in a jet plane, flying five miles high in the air and be served a delicious dinner. I just can't get over it, I'll be honest with you. It seems unbelievable. *Man* has done that, friend. Man is a very competent creature.

You can see what mankind would do with one language if they all came together against God.

So notice what God did—

> **Go to, let us go down, and there confound their language, that they may not understand one another's speech.**
>
> **So the LORD scattered them abroad from thence upon the face of all the earth: and they left off to build the city.**
>
> **Therefore is the name of it called Babel; because the LORD did there confound the language of all the earth: and from thence did the LORD scatter them abroad upon the face of all the earth [Gen. 11:7–9].**

Now man is scattered over the face of the earth. They were together in their rebellion, but now they can't understand one another. You know, a language barrier is a wall that is higher than the Wall of China. It is higher than the Berlin Wall and more effective. It is that which separates people, and it is stronger than any national border and any ocean.

There are a great many who say that languages developed gradually. But God said He confounded their language so that right then, while they were building, they suddenly couldn't understand each other. The building project came to a sudden halt, and folk moved away from Babel—they went in every direction.

This is a tremendous thing that took place. Here is a "speaking in tongues" when they couldn't understand each other. It is a miracle, a miracle of speaking and a miracle of hearing. They *spoke* different languages, and those who *heard* could not understand them.

Let me ask you a question: Was this a blessing in disguise, or was it a curse upon mankind? Well, for God's purposes it was a blessing. For man's development away from God, it was definitely a judgment. Down through the centuries mankind has been kept separate, and it has been a great hindrance to him. One thing that is happening today through the medium of radio and television and jet travel is that these walls are being broken down. They are tumbling down like the walls of Jericho. This is one reason that I believe God is coming down in judgment again.

Now let's put over against this tongues movement those events of the Day of Pentecost. That was another great tongues movement, and that time we find that the gospel was preached in all the languages that were understood by the people there. This was not speaking in an *unknown* tongue—that never was involved in the tongues movement to begin with. On the Day of Pentecost, God is giving His answer to the Tower of Babel. God is saying to mankind, "I have a gospel and a message for you, and I'm coming to you with the gospel in your own language."

This is the thing that God has done, and today the Bible has gone out in more languages than any other book. It is still being translated into tongues and dialects and is being brought to literally hundreds of tribes throughout the world. The gospel is for *all* mankind, and the reason and the purpose for the talking in tongues was to let the human race know that God had answered the Tower of Babel. He had a redemption for man now. The mission has been accomplished. It is no longer necessary for man to *try* to work out his salvation. He can listen to God's message and turn to Him. The gospel is for *you*, whoever you are and whatever tongue you speak. It's for you. It's for all the nations of the world. We are told in the final book of the Bible that there will be gathered into His presence ". . . a great multitude, which no man could number, of all nations, and kindreds, and people, and tongues . . ." (Rev. 7:9).

FROM SHEM TO ABRAHAM

Now we will take up the line of Shem since it is the line which will be followed throughout the Old Testament.

> **These are the generations of Shem: Shem was an hundred years old, and begat Arphaxad two years after the flood [Gen. 11:10].**

Shem's genealogy is given in the following verses, then we read:

> **And Nahor lived nine and twenty years, and begat Terah:**

> **And Nahor lived after he begat Terah an hundred and nineteen years, and begat sons and daughters [Gen. 11:24–25].**

You see that we are following the line of Terah. Why Terah? Notice the next verse:

> **And Terah lived seventy years, and begat Abram, Nahor, and Haran [Gen. 11:26].**

Now we are going to follow the line of Abram, whom we know as Abraham.

We're following the line of Shem, and we are actually going right through the Bible following this line. The Word of God will follow this line directly to the Cross of Christ. God has recorded all of this as preliminary. God now has demonstrated to man that he is in sin. In the incident of Cain and Abel, we find that Cain would not acknowledge that he was a sinner. In him we see a demonstration of the pride of life. At the Flood we see the sin of the *flesh* because the people then were given over to the sins of the flesh. They were indulging in violence and their every thought and imagination was evil. They were blind to their need of God. They were deaf to His claim, dead to God, dead in trespasses and sins. God gave them an invitation through

Noah. They spurned the invitation and remained in the sins of the flesh. Then, here at the Tower of Babel, we see the sin of the *will*, rebellion against God. That was the Tower of Babel.

Do you have your own little Tower of Babel which you have built? Are you in rebellion against God? Well, it is natural for human nature to be in rebellion against God.

Little Willie was being very cantankerous one evening. He was really cutting up, and his mother was having a great deal of trouble with him. Finally, she had to get him and put him in a corner—sat him down with his face to the wall and told him to sit there. She left him and went back to the living room with the rest of the family. After awhile she heard a noise in there, and she called to him, "Willie, are you standing up?" He said, "No, Mom, I'm sitting down, but I am standing up on the inside of me!"

Well, believe me, there are a lot of men and women in our day who are standing up on the inside of them, standing against God. They have built their own little Tower of Babel.

Now as we follow the line which is going to lead to Christ, here are the generations or the families of Terah—

> **Now these are the generations of Terah: Terah begat Abram, Nahor, and Haran; and Haran begat Lot.**
>
> **And Haran died before his father Terah in the land of his nativity, in Ur of the Chaldees.**
>
> **And Abram and Nahor took them wives: the name of Abram's wife was Sarai; and the name of Nahor's wife, Milcah, the daughter of Haran, the father of Milcah, and the father of Iscah.**
>
> **But Sarai was barren; she had no child.**
>
> **And Terah took Abram his son, and Lot the son of Haran his son's son, and Sarai his daughter in law, his son Abram's wife; and they went forth with them from Ur of the Chaldees, to go into the land of Canaan; and they came unto Haran, and dwelt there [Gen. 11:27–31].**

The name *Haran* means delay.

And the days of Terah were two hundred and five years: and Terah died in Haran [Gen. 11:32].

This bit of history is given to let us know that we are going to follow Abraham, and his story will begin in the next chapter.

It is at this point that the Book of Genesis—and, for that matter, the Bible as a whole—takes a turn. There is a great Grand Canyon which goes right down through the Book of Genesis. The first eleven chapters are on one side, and the last thirty-nine chapters are on the other side. In the first eleven chapters we cover over 2,000 years, as long a period as the rest of the Bible put together. Contrast that 2,000 years with the 350 years from Genesis 12 through 50. In these first eleven chapters of Genesis we have seen the Creation, the fall of man, the Flood, and the Tower of Babel. These are four great events which covered that long span of years.

CHAPTER 12

THEME: God's call and promise to Abraham; Abraham's response; Abraham's lapse of faith

The chapter before us brings us to the other side of the Grand Canyon which runs through Genesis. The atmosphere is altogether different here, and we are going to slow down to a walk. The emphasis turns from events, stupendous events, to personalities—not all of them were great but all of them were important personalities. In Genesis there are four, and others will follow in subsequent books of the Bible.

In the first eleven chapters we have seen four great events: the Creation, the fall of man, the Flood, and the Tower of Babel. In all of these tremendous events God has been dealing with the human race as a whole. Other than Adam and Abraham, God did not appear to anyone else. God was dealing with the entire race of mankind. There is a radical change at chapter 12. Now there will be brought before us four individuals. God will no longer be dealing with events, but with a man, and from that man He will make a nation. In the first section we will see Abraham the man of faith (Gen. 12—23). Then there will be Isaac the beloved son (Gen. 24—26). Next there will be Jacob the chosen and chastened son (Gen. 27—36), and then there will be Joseph's suffering and glory (Gen. 37—50). These four patriarchs are extremely important to the understanding of the Word of God. We will be taking up their stories in the rest of the Book of Genesis.

You see, God has demonstrated that He can no longer deal with the race. After the fall of man, we see the great sin of Cain. What was his great sin? *Pride.* He was angry because of the fact that deep down in his heart he was *proud* of the offering he had brought to God. And when his offering was rejected while his brother's was accepted, it caused him to *hate* his brother. His hatred led to murder, and the root of all of it was pride. Let me remind you that pride was also Satan's sin. Pride is the sin of the mind.

Then at the time of the Flood, the sin was the lust of the flesh. We saw that the actions and even the imaginations of man were to satisfy the flesh.

God had to bring the Flood to judge man at the time He did, because there was only one believer left—Noah. If God had waited even another generation, He would have lost the entire human race. God had certainly been patient with the world. He had waited 969 years, the entire life span of Methuselah. I am confident that you would say that 969 years is long enough to give anybody an opportunity to change his mind. But instead of turning to God, the people were in open rebellion, asserting a will that was against God. Following the Flood, the Tower of Babel reveals that "none seeketh after God."

After the Tower of Babel, God turns from the race of mankind to one individual. From that individual He is going to bring a nation, and to that nation He will give His revelation, and out of that nation He will bring the Redeemer. Apparently, this is the only way that God could do it. Or let me put it like this: If there were other ways, this was the *best* way. We can trust God to do the thing which is the best.

When God chose Abraham, He chose a man of faith. Abraham, by any person's measuring rod, is a great man. He is one of the greatest men who ever lived on this earth. How do you measure great men even today? Well, to begin with, the man has to be famous, and certainly Abraham measures up to that. He is probably the world's most famous man. Even in this day of radio and television, probably more people have heard of Abraham than of anyone else. More have heard of Abraham than have heard of the President of the United States, or of any head of state, or of any movie star, or of any athlete. The three great religions of the world go back to Abraham: Judaism, Islam, and Christianity. There are literally millions of people in Asia and Africa today who have heard of Abraham but have never heard of the ones who make the headlines in our country. One of the marks of a great man is fame; Abraham was a great man.

Another mark of a great man is that he must be noble of character, a generous man. Can you imagine anyone more generous than Abraham? I doubt whether there is a man alive who would do what he did. When he and his nephew came back into the land of Palestine, he told

Lot to choose any portion that he wanted, and Abraham said he would take what was left. Do you think any man would do that in a business deal today? They don't even do that in a church, friend, much less in a hard-boiled business world. But Abraham was a generous man. Have you ever noticed how generous he was with the kings of Sodom and Gomorrah? He told them he wouldn't take the booty, not even so much as a shoestring, because God was the One to whom he was looking.

Thirdly, a great man must live in a momentous time. He must be, as Napoleon said, a man of destiny. The man and the right time must meet at the crossroads of life. That was certainly true of Abraham.

I believe the world would agree with me on the first three points we have mentioned. They might not agree with this one: The fourth essential of a great man is that he must be a man of faith. You will notice that all great men, even when they are not Christian, have something in which they believe. God said that Abraham was a man of faith. In the Bible record the greatest thing that is said about Abraham is that he believed God: ". . . Abraham believed God, and it was counted unto him for righteousness" (Rom. 4:3). As we go through these chapters in Genesis, we will find that God appeared to this man seven times, each time to develop faith in his life. This does not mean that he was perfect. The fact of the matter is that he failed many times. God gave him four tests, and he fell flat on his face on all four of them. But, like Simon Peter, he got up, brushed himself off and started again. May I say to you, if God has touched your heart and life, you also may fall, but you are surely going to get up and start over again. We will see this happen in Abraham's life as we go through the chapter before us.

GOD'S CALL AND PROMISE TO ABRAHAM

The first three verses give us the threefold promise of God to Abraham (Abram), and actually this is the hub of the Bible. The rest of Scripture is an unfolding of this threefold promise.

Now the Lord had said unto Abram, Get thee out of thy country, and from thy kindred, and from thy father's house, unto a land that I will shew thee:

And I will make of thee a great nation, and I will bless thee, and make thy name great; and thou shalt be a blessing:

And I will bless them that bless thee, and curse him that curseth thee: and in thee shall all families of the earth be blessed [Gen. 12:1–3].

The first of the threefold promise is the *land*. God says, "I am going to show you a land, and I am going to give it to you." The second part of the promise is the *nation*—"I will make of thee a great nation, and I will bless thee, and make thy name great." He also promises him, "And I will bless them that bless thee, and curse him that curseth thee." The third part of the promise is that He would make him a *blessing*: "In thee shall all families of the earth be blessed." This is God's threefold promise.

Now the question arises: Has God made good on His promises to Abraham? God has certainly brought from him a great nation, and it has probably the longest tenure as a nation of any people on this earth. No one can quite match them.

How about the second promise—has Abraham been a blessing to all mankind? Yes, through the Lord Jesus Christ he has been a blessing to the whole world. Also the entire Word of God has come to us through Abraham.

God has fulfilled all His promises to Abraham—except the first one. God had said, "Abraham, I'm going to give you that land." And look at what is happening over there in our day. They are holding on to the land by their toenails, but they don't *have* it. Somebody says, "God didn't make that good." Well, let's not put it that way, my friend. Let's give God a chance. Two-thirds of the promise has been made good right to the very letter. But God said that He would not let them be in the land if they were disobedient and if they were away from Him. And they *are* away from Him today. As a result they are having trouble over there. Don't say that *God* is not making good His promise. The fact of the matter is that God is doing exactly what He said He would do. The day will come when God will put the people of Israel back in the land, and when He does it, they won't have only a toehold. They will have the land all the way east to the Euphrates River and all the way north as far as the Hittite nation was and all the way south to the river of Egypt, which is a little river in the Arabian desert. They have never really occupied the land God gave to them. At the zenith of their power, they occupied 30,000 square miles, but that is not all that God gave them. Actually, He gave them 300,000 square miles. They have a long way to go, but they will have to get it on God's terms and in God's appointed time. The United Nations can't do anything about it, and neither the United States nor Russia can settle their problem.

My friend, it is very comfortable today where I sit. I have come to the position that God is running things. It is nice to sit here without being frightened by the headlines in the newspaper and without being disturbed by what is going on in the world. God is in control, and He is going to work things out His way.

Now in the light of God's three promises to Abraham, what did he do?

ABRAHAM'S RESPONSE

In verse 1 we read: "Now the LORD had said unto Abram." We know from other Scriptures that God had called Abram when he lived in Ur of the Chaldees: "The God of glory appeared unto our father Abraham, when he was in Mesopotamia, before he dwelt in Charran, and said unto him, Get thee out of thy country, and from thy kindred, and come into the land which I shall shew thee. Then came he out of the Chaldeans, and dwelt in Charran: and from thence, when his father was dead, he removed him into this land, wherein ye now dwell" (Acts 7:2–4). Abraham obeyed God by leaving his home, his business, and the high civilization of Ur, "not knowing whither he went." Yet it was not complete obedience because we read that he took with him some of his family. He took with him his father, Terah, and God had told Abraham not to take him. Why was it that God wanted to get him out of the land and away from his relatives? We learn the answer in the Book of Joshua. ". . . Your fathers dwelt on the other side of the flood in old time, even Terah, the father of Abraham, and the father of Nachor; and they served other gods" (Josh. 24:2). They served other gods—Abraham was an idolator. The world was pretty far gone at that time. God had to move like this if He was going to save humanity. The other alternative for Him was to blot them all out and start over again. I'm glad He didn't do that. If He had, I wouldn't have been here, because I arrived here a *sinner*. The fact of the matter is, all sinners would have been blotted out. Thank God, He is a God of mercy and grace, and He saves sinners.

We'll follow the Scripture text now and call him Abram until chapter 17 where God changes his name to Abraham.

> **So Abram departed, as the LORD had spoken unto him; and Lot went with him: and Abram was seventy and five years old when he departed out of Haran [Gen. 12:4].**

"So Abram departed, as the LORD had spoken unto him." Now he will follow God's leading to the land of Canaan.

"And Lot went with him"—oh, oh! It is still incomplete obedience; he is taking his nephew Lot with him.

> **And Abram took Sarai his wife, and Lot his brother's son, and all their substance that they had gathered, and the souls that they had gotten in Haran; and they went forth to go into the land of Canaan; and into the land of Canaan they came [Gen. 12:5].**

Abram took Sarai, his wife, and that was all right, of course.

"And Lot his brother's son, and all their substance that they had gathered, and the souls that they had gotten in Haran." The time Abram had spent in Haran was a period of just marking time and of delaying the blessing of God. God never appeared to him again until he had moved into the land of Palestine, until he had separated at least from his closer relatives and brought only Lot with him.

"And into the land of Canaan they came"—now verse 6:

And Abram passed through the land unto the place of Sichem, unto the plain of Moreh. And the Canaanite was then in the land [Gen. 12:6].

Here is the record of the fact that the Canaanites were the descendants of Ham's son Canaan. I want to add something very important right at this point. A great many people think that Abram left a terrible place in Ur of the Chaldees and came to a land of corn and wine, a land of milk and honey, where everything was lovely. They think that Abram really bettered his lot by coming to this land. Don't you believe it. That is not what the Bible says. And through archaeology we know that Ur of the Chaldees had a very high civilization during this time. In fact, Abram and Sarai might well have had a bathtub in their home! Ur was a great and prosperous city. Abram left all of that and came into the land of Canaan, "and the Canaanite was then in the land." The Canaanite was not civilized; he was a barbarian and a heathen, if there ever was one. Abram's purpose in coming to Canaan was certainly not to better his lot. He came in obedience to God's command.

Now he has obeyed, and notice what happens—

And the LORD appeared unto Abram, and said, Unto thy seed will I give this land: and there builded he an altar unto the LORD, who appeared unto him [Gen. 12:7].

Abram builds an altar unto the Lord when He appears to him this second time. While he was in Haran, the place of delay, God had not appeared to him.

You see, one of the reasons that you and I are not always blessed in the reading of the Bible is because the Bible condemns—we are not living up to the light which God has already given to us. If we would obey God, then more blessing would come. We see in Abram's experience that God did not appear again to him until after he had moved out and had begun to obey God on the light that he had. Now God appears to him again. Then Abram builds an altar, and we will see that he is a real altar-builder.

And he removed from thence unto a mountain on the east of Beth-el, and pitched his tent, having Beth-el on the west, and Hai, on the east: and there he builded an altar unto the LORD, and called upon the name of the LORD [Gen. 12:8].

Abram does two things when he gets into the land. He pitches his tent—that is like buying a home in a new subdivision and moving in. He "pitched his tent"—that's where he lived. Then "he builded an altar." That was his testimony to God, and everywhere Abram went, he left a testimony to God.

My friend, what kind of a testimony do you have? To have a testimony, you don't need to leave tracts in front of your house and you don't have to have a "Jesus Saves" bumper sticker on your car (then drive like a maniac down the freeway, as some folk do). That is no testimony at all. May I say to you that Abram quietly worshiped God, and the Canaanites soon learned that he was a man who worshiped the Lord God.

And Abram journeyed, going on still toward the south [Gen. 12:9].

South is the right direction to go for warmer weather; so this man is moving south. He has itchy feet. He's a nomad.

Now we come to the blot in his life, actually the second one.

ABRAHAM'S LAPSE OF FAITH

And there was a famine in the land: and Abram went down into Egypt to sojourn there; for the famine was grievous in the land [Gen. 12:10].

Abram was in the land, and this was the place of blessing. God never told him to leave. But a famine was in the land, and I think one morning Abram pushed back the flap of his tent, looked out, and said, "Sarai, it looks like everybody's going to Egypt. There's a famine, you know, and it's getting worse. Maybe we ought to think about going down." And I suppose Sarai said, "Anything you want to do, Abram. I'm your wife and I'll go with you." After a few days had gone by and Abram had talked to some of these travelers (probably coming from north of where he was living and bringing the news that the famine was getting worse and was moving south) I imagine that he said to Sarai one evening, "I think we had better pack up and go to Egypt." So Abram and Sarai start down to Egypt.

Notice that *God* had not told him to do that. When God had appeared to him the last time, He had said, "This is *it*, Abram, this is the land I am going to give you. You will be a blessing, and I am going to bless you here." But, you see, Abram didn't believe God. He went down into the land of Egypt. In the Bible, Egypt is a picture of the world. You will find that all the way through. I think it is still a picture of the world—this was my opinion of it when I was there. But Abram went down to Egypt.

It's amazing how the world draws Christians today. So many of them rationalize. They'll say, "You know, brother McGee, we're not able to come to church on Sunday night because we have to get up and go to work Monday morning." Well, almost everybody has to do that. And it's amazing that those same people can go to a banquet on a week night and sit through a long-winded program with lots of music and lots of talk and not worry about getting up for work the next morning. It's amazing how the world draws Christians today and how they can rationalize.

I think that if you had met Abram going down to Egypt and had said, "Wait a minute, Abram, you're going the wrong direction—you should be staying in the land," that Abram could have given you a very good reason. He might have said, "Look, my sheep are getting pretty thin and there's not any pasture for them. Since there's plenty of grazing land for them down in Egypt, we're going down there." And that's where they went.

However, immediately there is a problem, and it concerns Sarai because she is a beautiful woman.

And it came to pass, when he was come near to enter
into Egypt, that he said unto Sarai his wife, Behold now,
I know that thou art a fair woman to look upon:

Therefore it shall come to pass, when the Egyptians
shall see thee, that they shall say, This is his wife: and
they will kill me, but they will save thee alive [Gen.
12:11–12].

As you probably know, over along the northwest shore of the Dead
Sea, ancient scrolls were found in the caves there, and they are known
as the Dead Sea Scrolls. At first the unbelieving scholars thought that
they had found something that would disprove the Bible. But have
you noticed how silent the higher critics have become? They just
don't seem to have found anything that contradicts the Bible.

Among the scrolls was a set which couldn't be unrolled because
they were so fragile—they had been wrapped so long that they would
just shatter and come to pieces. One name could be seen, the name
Lamech, so they were called part of the book of Lamech and said to be
one of the apocryphal books of the Bible. Boy, how incorrect that was!
The nation Israel bought them, and in the museum the experts began
to moisten and soften them until they were unrolled. The scholars
found that they contained Genesis 12, 13, 14, and 15, not in the Bible
text but rather an interpretation of it. In the part that deals with chapter 12, it tells about the beauty of Sarai, actually describing her features and telling how beautiful she was. It confirms what we read of
her in the Word of God.

The same scroll gives a description of Abram's exploration after
God told him to "walk through the land in the length of it and in the
breadth of it" (Gen. 13:17). The scroll gives a first person account by
Abram of his journey. It confirms what the Bible has said about the
land's beauty and fertility. The eyewitness (whether or not it was
really Abram, we do not know) certainly confirmed the Bible record.
A great many people who visit that land today can't understand how
it could be called a land of milk and honey. Well, in the Book of Deu-

teronomy we learn what caused the desolation that is seen there today. But it was a glorious land in Abram's day.

However, there were periods of famine, and Abram left the land and went down to Egypt during such a time.

As Abram neared Egypt, he recognized that he would get into difficulty because of the beauty of his wife. So he said to Sarai,

> **Say, I pray thee, thou art my sister: that it may be well with me for thy sake; and my soul shall live because of thee [Gen. 12:13].**

"Say, I pray thee, thou art my sister." That was half a lie, as we shall see. Half a lie is sometimes worse than a whole lie, and it certainly was intended to deceive. Abram's fears were well founded because Pharaoh did take Sarai. We know from the Book of Esther that in those days there was a period of preparation for a woman to become a wife of a ruler. And during that period of preparation, God "plagued Pharaoh and his house with great plagues," and let him know that he was not to take Sarai as his wife.

> **And Pharaoh called Abram, and said, What is this that thou hast done unto me? why didst thou not tell me that she was thy wife?**
>
> **Why saidst thou, She is my sister? so I might have taken her to me to wife: now therefore behold thy wife, take her, and go thy way.**
>
> **And Pharaoh commanded his men concerning him: and they sent him away, and his wife, and all that he had [Gen. 12:18–20].**

God, you see, was overruling in the lives of Abram and Sarai, but God did not *appear* to him while he was in the land of Egypt.

CHAPTER 13

THEME: Abraham separates from Lot; Lot goes to
Sodom; God appears to Abraham and reaffirms
His promise

In chapter 13 we see the return of Abram from the land of Egypt.
Abram and Lot leave Egypt and return to the Land of Promise. Lot
separates from Abram and goes to Sodom, and then God appears to
Abram for the third time. As long as Abram is in the land of Egypt and
as long as he is still holding on to Lot, God does not appear to him.
The minute that he comes back to the land and there is the separation
from Lot, God appears to him.

ABRAHAM SEPARATES FROM LOT

**And Abram went up out of Egypt, he, and his wife, and
all that he had, and Lot with him, into the south.**

**And Abram was very rich in cattle, in silver, and in gold
[Gen. 13:1–2].**

Abram was the John D. Rockefeller of that day. He was a very wealthy
man at this time.

**And he went on his journeys from the south even to
Beth-el, unto the place where his tent had been at the
beginning, between Beth-el and Hai [Gen. 13:3].**

Abram went far north of Jerusalem. He had come to the south, around
Hebron, and now he goes north of Jerusalem to Bethel.

**Unto the place of the altar, which he had made there at
the first: and there Abram called on the name of the
LORD [Gen. 13:4].**

Although he may stumble and fall, this man comes back to God. There is always a way back to the altar for Abram, the prodigal son, and any man or woman who wants to come back to God. The arms of the Father are open to receive them.

And Lot also, which went with Abram, had flocks, and herds, and tents [Gen. 13:5].

Lot did pretty well down in the land of Egypt also.

And the land was not able to bear them, that they might dwell together: for their substance was great, so that they could not dwell together.

And there was a strife between the herdmen of Abram's cattle and the herdmen of Lot's cattle: and the Canaanite and the Perizzite dwelled then in the land [Gen. 13:6–7].

The Word of God is a marvelous Word if you just let it speak to you. Will you notice this: Abram got two things in the land of Egypt which caused him untold grief. One was riches, and the second was a little Egyptian maid by the name of Hagar. We will see more about her later. But now he has riches, and it causes him and Lot to have to separate—there is strife between them.

Did you notice this statement: "And the Canaanite and the Perizzite dwelled then in the land"? Abram's herdsmen and Lot's herdsmen are fighting, and then Abram and Lot disagree. The very interesting thing is that then the Canaanite probably whispered over to the Perizzite, "Look at them! Fightin' again! When they came into this land and built an altar to the living and true God, how we looked up to Abram! When he first came here, we thought he was such a wonderful man. We knew he was honest, we knew he was truthful, but look at him now. Look at the strife they're having!" I do not think the Perizzite and the Canaanite were very well impressed by Abram and Lot at this time.

Let me say this to you, although it may step on your toes. I do not know your town, I do not know where you live, but if yours is like other towns and like the town I came from, the Methodists and the Baptists and the Presbyterians don't get along, and there is fighting. And when there are these internal fights in a church today, the unsaved man on the outside knows about it. May I say to you, he then says, "If that's Christianity, I don't want any part of it. I can get a fight outside. I don't need to join the church to get a fight." The Lord Jesus did not say to His own, nor to the church today, "By this shall all men know that you are My disciples if you're fundamental and you organize a church." Oh, no! He said, "By this shall all men know that ye are my disciples, if ye have love one to another" (John 13:35). The "Perizzite" and the "Canaanite"—those old rascals—know when your church is fighting on the inside, my friend.

I had an uncle who never came to know the Lord. My aunt used to weep and say, "Oh, he won't listen!" Do you know why? With her lived a sister, another aunt, and I used to go there sometimes on Sundays for dinner. Do you know what we had for dinner? Roast preacher! One of my aunts went to the Methodist church, the other went to the Presbyterian church, and oh, boy, did they try to outdo each other, talking about the preacher and the fights that were going on. I used to watch my uncle. He would just sit there and eat. Then he'd get up to leave and go down to his club for the afternoon. When he would come home in the evening, he wasn't drunk, but he sure had had several drinks. They never won him to Christ. There are a lot of people not being won today, my friend, because of the strife that is inside the church. This is an interesting thing: "the Canaanite and the Perizzite dwelled then in the land." And they still dwell in the land. They are right near your church, by the way.

And Abram said unto Lot, Let there be no strife, I pray thee, between me and thee, and between my herdmen and thy herdmen; for we be brethren.

Is not the whole land before thee? separate thyself, I pray thee, from me: if thou wilt take the left hand, then I will go to the right; or if thou depart to the right hand, then I will go to the left [Gen. 13:8–9].

It is Abram who makes the division. It took a big man to tell Lot this. In other words, Abram is saying that Lot could choose what he wanted and Abram would take what was left.

LOT GOES TO SODOM

And Lot lifted up his eyes, and beheld all the plain of Jordan, that it was well watered every where, before the Lord destroyed Sodom and Gomorrah, even as the garden of the Lord, like the land of Egypt, as thou comest unto Zoar [Gen. 13:10].

That was a beautiful spot in those days.

Then Lot chose him all the plain of Jordan; and Lot journeyed east: and they separated themselves the one from the other.

Abram dwelled in the land of Canaan, and Lot dwelled in the cities of the plain, and pitched his tent toward Sodom [Gen. 13:11–12].

This is interesting. Probably during all the time Lot spent in that land with Abram, at night he would push back the flap of his tent and look out and say to Mrs. Lot, "Isn't that a beautiful spot down there?" In the morning he would get up and say, "My, it looks so attractive down there!" The grass is always greener in the other pasture. When the day came that Lot could make a decision and go, you know the direction he went. No man falls suddenly. It always takes place over a period of time. You lift the flap of your tent, and you pitch your tent toward Sodom—and that's the beginning. Lot lifted up his eyes, he saw the plain, and he headed in that direction. That is the biggest mistake he ever made in his life.

Lot did not know this:

But the men of Sodom were wicked and sinners before the Lord exceedingly [Gen. 13:13].

We will see later what happened to Lot and Mrs. Lot and the family down in Sodom.

GOD APPEARS TO ABRAHAM AND REAFFIRMS HIS PROMISE

And the Lord said unto Abram, after that Lot was separated from him, Lift up now thine eyes, and look from the place where thou art northward, and southward, and eastward, and westward [Gen. 13:14].

"And the Lord said unto Abram, after that Lot was separated from him"—here is the third appearance of God to this man.

"Lift up now thine eyes, and look from the place where thou art northward, and southward, and eastward, and westward." This is the land God is going to give him. As God continued to appear to Abram and later on to the other patriarchs, God put sideboards around that land. In other words, He put a border to it and told them exactly what the land was. He was very specific about it.

May I just interject this thought? This ought to get rid of that song, "Beautiful Isle of Somewhere." If there ever was a song that needed *not* to be sung at a funeral, that is the one. Can you imagine Abram looking northward, eastward, southward, and westward and singing "Beautiful Isle of Somewhere" when he was standing right in the middle of it? Heaven is a real place as truly as the Promised Land is a real place—*not* a beautiful isle of somewhere. It is a very definite place about which the Word of God is quite specific. In the Book of Revelation God makes it so specific; He puts the boundary right around it, and we can know something about it. God does not deal with that which is theoretical, but with that which is actual and real.

For all the land which thou seest, to thee will I give it, and to thy seed for ever.

And I will make thy seed as the dust of the earth: so that if a man can number the dust of the earth, then shall thy seed also be numbered [Gen. 13:15–16].

Notice what God does for this man. He labels the land and tells Abram that he is in it. He also again confirms the fact that Abram is going to have a tremendous offspring—which he has had.

Arise, walk through the land in the length of it and in the breadth of it; for I will give it unto thee [Gen. 13:17].

It is very interesting that one of the Dead Sea Scrolls describes this particular section of Genesis, and it gives a first-person account by Abraham of the land. It was a wonderful land in that day.

Then Abram removed his tent, and came and dwelt in the plain of Mamre, which is in Hebron, and built there an altar unto the LORD [Gen. 13:18].

Abram was quite an altar builder. You could always tell where Abram had been because he left a testimony. Man has left a footprint on the moon. They've left a flag up there and a little motto saying, "We have come in peace"—but they did not leave the Bible, the Word of God. That reveals the difference between the thinking of Abram and the thinking of the age and period in which we live today. The important thing to Abram was an altar to the Lord, and that is exactly what he built.

One of the meanings of *Mamre* is "richness," and *Hebron* means "communion." That is a marvelous place to dwell. In our day we can be fairly certain that we have located the tree where Abram was, and the well that is there—I have been there. It is quite an interesting spot between Hebron and Mamre, and that is where Abram dwelt. It is a good place to be: in the place of richness and of communion with God. This seems to have been Abram's home, and this is where he is buried.

CHAPTER 14

THEME: Kings of the east capture Sodom and Gomorrah; Abraham delivers Lot; Abraham refuses booty

In chapter 14 we find the first recorded war, one in which Abram delivers Lot; and we find the appearance of the first priest, at which time Abram is blessed by Melchizedek. These are the two great truths that are here. In one sense, this is a most remarkable chapter. It does not seem to fit in with the story at all. It seems that it could be left out, that there is a continuity without it. But it is one of the most important chapters in the Book of Genesis.

KINGS OF THE EAST
CAPTURE SODOM AND GOMORRAH

And it came to pass in the days of Amraphel king of Shinar, Arioch king of Ellasar, Chedorlaomer king of Elam, and Tidal king of nations;

That these made war with Bera king of Sodom, and with Birsha king of Gomorrah, Shinab king of Admah, and Shemeber king of Zeboiim, and the king of Bela, which is Zoar [Gen. 14:1–2].

First of all, let me say that this is a historical document. In the first eleven verses, it is recorded that the kings of the east defeat the kings of Sodom and Gomorrah. For quite a few years, the critical, radical scholars rejected this, saying that these men's names do not appear in secular history at all and that this is a rather ridiculous story. But did you know that the names of these kings have been found on monuments and tablets, showing that they did exist? In fact, Amraphel is now known to be the Hammurabi of other secular history. The record that we have here is tremendously significant.

There was war, and this is the first war that is mentioned in Scripture. Mankind began early in making war. Although this is the first war recorded, I do not know that it is the first war that ever took place—I do not think that the writer intends to give that impression. The reason it is recorded is because Lot, the nephew of Abram, is involved.

All these were joined together in the vale of Siddim, which is the salt sea.

Twelve years they served Chedorlaomer, and in the thirteenth year they rebelled [Gen. 14:3–4].

The rebellion is what brought the kings of the east against Sodom and Gomorrah. These kings evidently had fought before, because the kings of the east had subjugated these cities of the plain, but the cities had reached the place of rebellion. In verses 5–11 we read the account of how the kings of the east overcame the kings who had joined together around the lower part of the Dead Sea.

And they took Lot, Abram's brother's son, who dwelt in Sodom, and his goods, and departed [Gen. 14:12].

Lot lived in Sodom and was taken captive. The reason this war is significant to the record here is that it reveals what Abram is going to do in connection with his nephew.

ABRAHAM DELIVERS LOT

And there came one that had escaped, and told Abram the Hebrew; for he dwelt in the plain of Mamre the Amorite, brother of Eschol, and brother of Aner: and these were confederate with Abram [Gen. 14:13].

When the kings of the east left the area of Sodom and Gomorrah with their captives, they moved north along the west bank of the Dead Sea, which was not too far from Hebron and Mamre where Abram was dwelling. You can stand where Abram stood in that day and see any movement that takes place down toward the Dead Sea. So that when word was brought to Abram, he immediately began to pursue the enemy as he moved north.

"And these were confederate with Abram." Notice that Abram has a group of men that are with him. They had to stand together in that day because of the pursuit or the approach of an enemy. They either had to hang together or hang separately.

> **And when Abram heard that his brother was taken captive, he armed his trained servants, born in his own house, three hundred and eighteen, and pursued them unto Dan [Gen. 14:14].**

This is startling, and it reveals something of the extent of Abram's possessions. This gives you some conception of the number of servants Abram had. In his own household, he could arm 318. How many did he have that he could not arm? For instance, there would also be women and children and the old folk—but he could arm 318. To have that many hired hands indicates that Abram was carrying on quite a business of raising cattle and sheep.

"And pursued them unto Dan"—Dan is up in the north.

> **And he divided himself against them, he and his servants, by night, and smote them, and pursued them unto Hobah, which is on the left hand of Damascus [Gen. 14:15].**

Abram pursued these men all the way north to Damascus—that is quite a stretch. Apparently, what Abram did was to divide his servants. One group made an attack, probably from the rear as they were pursuing them. The other group went around, and when the enemy turned to fight the first group, the second group came down upon them. As a result, Abram was able to get a victory. At least he was able

to scatter them so that they fled across the desert, leaving the people
and the booty they had captured.

**And he brought back all the goods, and also brought
again his brother Lot, and his goods, and the women
also, and the people [Gen. 14:16].**

You see that they were taking the women and the other people as
slaves. Abram has done a tremendous thing, and he has done it because of his nephew Lot. That is the reason all of this is mentioned
here. This is very definitely not an extraneous chapter. It is a part of
the life of Abram, and it is very important.

**And the king of Sodom went out to meet him after his
return from the slaughter of Chedorlaomer, and of the
kings that were with him, at the valley of Shaveh, which
is the king's dale [Gen. 14:17].**

The king of Sodom went out to meet Abram. But now someone else is
going to come out and meet Abram, and it is a good thing that he did,
because the king of Sodom is going to put a grave temptation before
Abram.

**And Melchizedek king of Salem brought forth bread
and wine: and he was the priest of the most high God.**

**And he blessed him, and said, Blessed be Abram of the
most high God, possessor of heaven and earth [Gen.
14:18–19].**

I have several questions here, and I am sure that you do. To begin
with, where in the world did this man Melchizedek come from? He
just walks out on the page of Scripture with bread and wine, he
blesses Abram, and then he walks off the page of Scripture—that's it. I
wonder where he came from. I wonder where he is going, and I wonder what his business is.

I find out that he is king of Salem, but he is also priest of the most high God. But now I have another question: How did he find out about "the most high God"? He found out somewhere. *El Elohim* is the most high God, the Creator of heaven and earth; in other words, the living God, the God of Genesis 1, the God of Noah, and the God of Enoch. This is the One—He is *not* a local deity. H. C. Leupold in his book on Genesis says that this is "strictly a monotheistic conception." Dr. Samuel M. Zwemer, in his *Origin of Religion*, says that this reveals that there was monotheism before polytheism. In other words, all men had a knowledge of the living and true God. "Because that, when they knew God, they glorified him not as God, neither were thankful; but became vain in their imaginations, and their foolish heart was darkened" (Rom. 1:21). Paul goes on to say that men continued to go down to the point where they began to worship the creature more than the Creator.

Yet back in Abram's day here is a man who is high priest for the world of that day. He has a knowledge of the living and true God. He is a priest of the living and true God. He comes out, bringing bread and wine to Abram—those are the elements of the Lord's Supper! I wonder what he had in mind? How much did Melchizedek know?

Melchizedek is mentioned three times in Scripture. In addition to this passage in Genesis, he is also mentioned in Psalm 110:4, which is prophetic of Christ: ". . . Thou art a priest for ever after the order of Melchizedek." Finally, he is mentioned several times in Hebrews. After reading Hebrews, I know why nothing is said about his origin in Genesis. Nothing is said about his parents, and that is strange because the Book of Genesis is the book of families. It tells about the beginnings of these families. Every time we see mentioned a man who is important in the genealogical line (as this man Melchizedek's), his parents are mentioned. "He is the son of So-and-So," or "'these are the generations of So-and-So." But we do not have the generations of Melchizedek. The writer to the Hebrews makes it very clear that the reason there is no record of Melchizedek's father or mother or beginning or ending of days is because the priesthood of Christ, in its inception, is after the order of Melchizedek. In *service*—in what our Lord did in the sacrifice of Himself and in His entering the Holy of Holies, which is heaven today—Christ's priesthood follows the order of Aaron. But in His person, our Lord had no beginning or ending of days, and His priesthood follows the order of Melchizedek. As King, Christ is son of Abraham, He is son of David—the Gospel of Matthew tells us that. But in the Gospel of John we read: "In the beginning was the Word, and the Word was with God, and the Word was God. . . . And the Word was made flesh, and dwelt among us, (and we behold his glory, the glory as of the only begotten of the Father,) full of grace and truth" (John 1:1, 14). He had no beginning or ending of days as far as creation is concerned—He is the eternal God. He came out of heaven's glory, the Word was made flesh, and we beheld His glory. We have in Melchizedek a marvelous picture of the Lord Jesus Christ.

"Brought forth bread and wine." I know now why Melchizedek does this. It is because the Scriptures say, "For as often as ye eat this bread, and drink this cup, ye do shew the Lord's death till he come" (1 Cor. 11:26). Melchizedek is anticipating the death of Christ here!

On that basis he blessed Abram: "Blessed be Abram of the most high God, possessor of heaven and earth"—*El Elohim*, the Creator. This man was the high priest of the world in that day. The Lord Jesus is the great High Priest for the world today. The Lord Jesus is after the order of Melchizedek—not Aaron—as set forth here. Aaron was just for Israel and just for a tabernacle. In His person, Christ is after the order of Melchizedek.

And blessed be the most high God, which hath delivered thine enemies into thy hand. And he gave him tithes of all [Gen. 14:20].

Abram paid tithes to Melchizedek here at the very beginning. How did he know about paying tithes? Obviously, he had a revelation from God concerning this—as well as concerning other matters.

ABRAHAM REFUSES BOOTY

And the king of Sodom said unto Abram, Give me the persons, and take the goods to thyself [Gen. 14:21].

This is the temptation. According to the Code of Hammurabi of that day, this man Abram had a perfect right to the booty and even to the persons. But the king of Sodom is clever; he says, "Give us the persons, and you take the booty—it's yours." That was a temptation to Abram. Forever after, when anybody would say, "That man Abram is certainly a wealthy man. God has blessed him," I think that the king of Sodom would have said, "Blessed him, my foot! God didn't bless him. I gave it to him; I'm the one who made him rich!" Abram knew that. Listen to him now:

> **And Abram said to the king of Sodom, I have lift up mine hand unto the Lord, the most high God, the possessor of heaven and earth [Gen. 14:22].**

Abram is still under the influence and the blessing of Melchizedek, and it is a good thing he met Melchizedek. God always prepares us for any temptation that comes to us. He says that He will never let any temptation come to us that we are not able to bear (see 1 Cor. 10:13). God had prepared Abram for this one.

> **That I will not take from a thread even to a shoelatchet, and that I will not take any thing that is thine, lest thou shouldest say, I have made Abram rich [Gen. 14:23].**

When Abram started out, he made a covenant with God, probably saying, "Oh, God, I am not entering this war in order to get booty. I'm not after possessions. I want to restore and recover my nephew Lot." And God permitted him to do that. Now Abram tells this to the king of Sodom as a witness to him. Abram could have said, "I worship the living and the true God. I have taken an oath that I would not take anything. You can't make me rich. I won't let you give me a shoestring or a piece of thread because, if you did even that, you would run around and say that you made me rich. If I get rich, God will have to do it."

Save only that which the young men have eaten, and the portion of the men which went with me, Aner, Eschol, and Mamre; let them take their portion [Gen. 14:24].

But Abram says, "These other men have a right to the booty, and they can have it; but I am not taking anything. What the young men who are with me have eaten is their pay for serving you and delivering you. But as for me—you cannot give me a thing."

CHAPTER 15

THEME: God's revelation of Himself as shield and reward; Abraham's faith; God's covenant with Abraham

GOD'S REVELATION OF HIMSELF AS SHIELD AND REWARD

We come to one of the high points of the Bible here in chapter 15.

After these things the word of the LORD came unto Abram in a vision, saying, Fear not, Abram: I am thy shield, and thy exceeding great reward [Gen. 15:1].

This now is the fourth time that God has appeared to Abram. God is developing this man and bringing him farther along. God does well to appear to him now because Abram has taken a tremendous step of faith in going out and rescuing Lot and in turning down the booty which the king of Sodom offered him.

"Fear not, Abram: I am thy shield." My friend, this is lovely; this is wonderful. The record does not tell us this, but let me suggest to you that perhaps during the battle, Abram got in real danger and wondered whether he would come out of it alive. God simply reminds him, "I'm your shield, Abram. I'm your shield."

"And thy exceeding great reward." In other words, God says, "You did well to turn down the booty. I am your reward; I intend to reward you." Oh, what God can do with a man today when he is willing just to believe God and look to Him!

If you think Abram is one of these pious boys who gets his halo shined every morning, you are wrong. Abram is very practical, and he is going to get right down to the nitty-gritty now. I think that God likes us to do that. I wish that we could get rid of this false piosity and the hypocritical attitude that so many fundamentalists assume today. Notice what this man Abram says—it is quite wonderful:

> **And Abram said, Lord God, what wilt thou give me, seeing I go childless, and the steward of my house is this Eliezer of Damascus?**

> **And Abram said, Behold, to me thou hast given no seed: and, lo, one born in my house is mine heir [Gen. 15:2–3].**

What Abram is saying to God is this: "I don't want more riches; I don't need that. The thing that's on my heart is that I'm childless and I want a son. You have promised to make me a father of nations and that my offspring will be as numberless as the sand on the seashore. But I don't even have one child!" According to the law of the day, the Code of Hammurabi, Eliezer, his steward, his head servant, who had an offspring, would in time inherit if Abram did not have a child.

> **And, behold, the word of the Lord came unto him, saying, This shall not be thine heir; but he that shall come forth out of thine own bowels shall be thine heir [Gen. 15:4].**

God is very practical when a man will be practical with Him. He says, "I am going to give you a son, Abraham. I am going to give you a son."
Now God took Abram by the hand and brought him forth into the night.

> **And he brought him forth abroad, and said, Look now toward heaven, and tell the stars, if thou be able to number them: and he s id unto him, So shall thy seed be [Gen. 15:5].**

This is remarkable. First God said to him that his offspring would be as numberless as the sand on the seashore, and now He says they will be as numberless as the stars in heaven. Abram could not number the stars. He could see approximately four thousand, but there were probably over fifty thousand in that area where he was looking. Abram couldn't number his offspring, and you couldn't do it today.

This man Abram actually has two seeds. He has a physical seed, the nation Israel, and he has a spiritual seed, the church. How does the church become Abraham's spiritual seed? By faith. Paul told the Galatians that they were the sons of Abraham by faith in Jesus Christ—not in a natural line, but a spiritual seed (see Gal. 3:29).

I had the privilege of speaking to a group of very fine young Jewish men many years ago in Nashville, Tennessee. I had known some of them before I was saved and had been a very close friend of theirs. I spoke on the glories of the Mosaic Law and told them that the fulfillment of it was in Christ. I began by telling them I was glad to speak to them because I knew that they were sons of Abraham. But when I told them I was a son of Abraham also, they looked in amazement one to another. And then I told them how I was a son of Abraham. Included in God's promise were these two seeds of Abraham, and this is a very wonderful truth.

ABRAHAM'S FAITH

And he believed in the Lord; and he counted it to him for righteousness [Gen. 15:6].

This is one of the greatest statements in the Scriptures: "And he believed in the Lord." What this means is that Abram said amen to God. God has said, "I will do this for you," and Abram says to God, "I believe You. Amen. I believe it." And that was counted to him for righteousness.

Paul speaks of this in his Epistle to the Romans: "What shall we say then that Abraham our father, as pertaining to the flesh, hath found? For if Abraham were justified by works, he hath whereof to glory; but not before God. For what saith the scripture? Abraham believed God, and it was counted unto him for righteousness. Now to him that worketh is the reward not reckoned of grace, but of debt. But to him that worketh not, but believeth on him that justifieth the ungodly, his faith is counted for righteousness" (Rom. 4:1–5). "What shall we say

then that Abraham our father, as pertaining to the flesh, hath found"—
or, that Abraham has found as pertaining to the flesh. I think that re-
wording brings out the meaning better.

"For what saith the scripture? Abraham believed God, and it
[that is, his faith] was counted unto him for righteousness"—for that
is what it was *not*, but that is what God counted it.

"Now to him that worketh is the reward not reckoned of grace, but
of debt." If you can *work* for your salvation, then God *owes* it to you.
But, my friend, God never saves by any other means except grace. He
has never had any other method of saving, and if you ever get saved, it
will be because you believe God, you accept Christ as your Savior, and
you believe that God has provided salvation for you.

"But to him that worketh not [no works at all], but believeth on
him that justifieth the ungodly [What kind of folk? Ungodly folk.], his
faith is counted for righteousness." His faith is counted for what it is
not, that is, for righteousness.

Abraham just believed God. He just accepted what God said, and
he believed God. That is the way you get saved: to believe that God has
done something for you, that Christ died for you and rose again. God
will declare you righteous by simply accepting Christ.

In the third chapter of Galatians, we have this same great truth:
"Even as Abraham believed God, and it was accounted to him for
righteousness. Know ye therefore that they which are of faith, the
same are the children of Abraham. And the scripture, foreseeing that
God would justify the heathen through faith, preached before the gospel unto Abraham, saying, In thee shall all nations be blessed. So
then they which be of faith are blessed with faithful Abraham" (Gal.
3:6–9). The faith which Abraham had made him faithful to God, but
he was not saved by being faithful. He was saved by believing God.
This is all-important for us to see.

GOD'S COVENANT WITH ABRAHAM

**And he said unto him, I am the LORD that brought thee
out of Ur of the Chaldees, to give thee this land to inherit
it.**

And he said, LORD **God, whereby shall I know that I
shall inherit it? [Gen. 15:7–8].**

Again, Abram is a very practical man. He believes in dealing with
reality, and I think we need to do that. We need reality today in our
Christian lives. If reality is not in your life, there is nothing there. A
great many people just play church today. Abram is very practical. He
wants to know something, and he would like to have something in
writing.

Do you know what God is probably going to tell him? God is going
to say, "Abram, I'm glad you asked Me, because I am going to meet
you down at the courthouse; I will go before a notary public, and I will
make real this contract which I am making with you. You are going to
have a son. Meet Me down there, and I will sign on the dotted line."
Now, before you write me a letter and protest, let me say that you are
right, that the Bible says nothing about God meeting Abram at the
courthouse, and it says nothing about going to a notary public, but in
the terms of the law of our day, that is exactly what God said to Abram.

Here is what God told Abram to do:

**And he said unto him, Take me an heifer of three years
old, and a she goat of three years old, and a ram of three
years old, and a turtledove, and a young pigeon.**

**And he took unto him all these, and divided them in the
midst, and laid each piece one against another: but the
birds divided he not [Gen. 15:9–10].**

God told Abram to prepare a sacrifice. He was to get a heifer, a she
goat, and a ram and divide or split them down the middle and put one
half on one side and one half on the other. The turtledove and the
pigeon he did not divide, but put one over here and one over there.

When men made a contract in that day, this is the way they made it.
Suppose one man agreed to buy sheep from another one. They would
prepare a sacrifice in this manner. The party of the first part joined
hands with the party of the second part, they stated their contract,

and then they walked through the sacrifice. In that day this corresponded to going down to the courthouse and signing before a notary public in our day. So we see that God is using with Abram the legal procedure of his day.

In Jeremiah 34:18 we have a reference to this custom that was prevalent in that land, not just among these people, but among all peoples in the day: "And I will give the men that have transgressed my covenant, which have not performed the words of the covenant which they had made before me, when they cut the calf in twain, and passed between the parts thereof." The method in that day was to take the sacrifice and divide it, and the men would then make the contract.

Notice Abram got everything ready according to God's instructions.

And when the fowls came down upon the carcases, Abram drove them away [Gen. 15:11].

This is a very human scene. Abram gets everything ready, and while he is waiting for the Lord, the fowls of the air come down—the buzzard and the crow come down upon the carrion. Abram is there shooing them away, for they are ready to swoop down upon the sacrifice. If you had been there and had seen all this display of the sacrifices, knowing the custom of the day, you might have said, "Well, brother Abram, apparently the one you're making a contract with hasn't shown up. I guess he's late!" Abram would have said, "No, I don't think He's late. He just told me to get things ready and that He would be here to make the contract."

And when the sun was going down, a deep sleep fell upon Abram; and, lo, an horror of great darkness fell upon him [Gen. 15:12].

Abram is paralyzed in sleep and put aside. It seems very strange that God would paralyze him in sleep when he is supposed to be making a contract, but this is an unusual contract. God is going to go through the sacrifices because God is promising something, but Abram is not going to go through because Abram is not promising to do a thing. Abram just believed God—that's all.

That is exactly what took place over nineteen hundred years ago when God sent His Son. God the Father so loved the world that He gave His only begotten Son. And the Son agreed to come to the earth and die for the sins of the world—your sin and mine—that whosoever would believe in Him (simply accept His gift) might not perish but have everlasting life (see John 3:16). I wasn't even there nineteen hundred years ago to make a contract, but God the Father and God the Son were there, and the Son went to the Cross, and He died for my sins. I was paralyzed by sin. I could not promise anything, and you couldn't either.

Abram did not promise anything either. Suppose that God had said to Abram, "Abram if you will just promise to say your prayers every night, I am going to do this for you." And suppose Abram forgot to pray one night. The contract is shot—it's broken—and therefore God does not need to make His part good. But God said that He would do His part, and He is asking man to do just one thing: to say amen to Him—that is, to believe Him. You are to believe God and believe what He has done. My friend, to believe God is salvation.

Years ago there was a dear little Scottish mother whose son had gone away to college in Glasgow and had come back an unbeliever. She talked with the boy and told about how wonderful God was and that she was sure of her salvation. The son had become skeptical, and he was a little provoked. Finally he said, "How do you know you're saved? Your little soul doesn't amount to anything." He began to compare her to the vastness of the universe and said that God could forget all about her and she couldn't be sure of her salvation. She didn't say anything, but just kept serving the boy's breakfast. Finally, when she had finished, she sat down with him and said, "You know, son, I've been thinking about it. Maybe you're right. Maybe my little soul doesn't amount to much. Maybe in the vastness of God's universe, He wouldn't miss me at all. But if He doesn't save me, He's going to lose more than I'm going to lose. I would lose only my insignificant little soul, but He would lose His reputation because He *promised* to save my soul. He agreed to do it: 'that whosoever believeth in him should not perish, but have everlasting life.'" God is the One who went through; God made the contract.

> **And he said unto Abram, Know of a surety that thy seed shall be a stranger in a land that is not theirs, and shall serve them; and they shall afflict them four hundred years [Gen. 15:13].**

In the Scriptures it is predicted that the Hebrew people would be put out of the land three times. This is the first time. It is also predicted that they would return back to the land, and they did this time. Later on it was the Babylonian captivity. They were carried into captivity, and they returned. In A.D. 70 Jerusalem was destroyed, and for the third time they were scattered. They have never returned from that. Their current presence in the land is by no means a fulfillment of Scripture. But according to the Word of God, they will come back someday exactly as it predicts.

> **And also that nation, whom they shall serve, will I judge: and afterward shall they come out with great substance.**
>
> **And thou shalt go to thy fathers in peace; thou shalt be buried in a good old age [Gen. 15:14–15].**

They did come out of Egypt with great substance, but Abram would not live to see it, of course.

> **But in the fourth generation they shall come hither again; for the iniquity of the Amorites is not yet full [Gen. 15:16].**

God is saying to Abram, "I cannot put you in this land now because I love Amorites also, and I want to give them a chance to turn to Me." And God gave the Amorites four hundred years—that is a long time, is it not?—to see if they would turn to Him. The only one in that land who turned to Him was that Canaanite woman, Rahab the harlot. She turned to God; she believed Him. All God asks *you* to do is to believe Him. God gave the Amorites this great period of opportunity.

> **And it came to pass, that, when the sun went down, and it was dark, behold a smoking furnace, and a burning lamp that passed between those pieces [Gen. 15:17].**

Both of these speak of Christ. The furnace, of course, speaks of judgment. The lamp speaks of Him as the light of the world.

> **In the same day the LORD made a covenant with Abram, saying, Unto thy seed have I given this land, from the river of Egypt unto the great river, the river Euphrates:**
>
> **The Kenites, and the Kenizzites, and the Kadmonites,**
>
> **And the Hittites, and the Perizzites, and the Rephaims,**
>
> **And the Amorites, and the Canaanites, and the Girgashites, and the Jebusites [Gen. 15:18–21].**

God now marks out the land that He is promising to Abram. By the way, what did Abram promise to do? Nothing. He believed God. And God will save you—save you by grace—if you will believe what He has done for you.

BIBLIOGRAPHY
(Recommended for Further Study)

Barnhouse, Donald Grey. *Genesis: A Devotional Exposition.* Grand Rapids, Michigan: Zondervan Publishing House, 1973.

Borland, James A. *Christ in the Old Testament.* Chicago, Illinois: Moody Press, 1978.

Davis, John J. *Paradise to Prison: Studies in Genesis.* Grand Rapids, Michigan: Baker Book House, 1975.

DeHaan, M. R. *Genesis and Evolution.* Grand Rapids, Michigan: Zondervan Publishing House, 1962.

DeHaan, M. R. *The Days of Noah.* Grand Rapids, Michigan: Zondervan Publishing House, 1962.

Gispen, William Hendrik. *Genesis.* Grand Rapids, Michigan: Zondervan Publishing House, 1982.

Jensen, Irving L. *Genesis—A Self-Study Guide.* Chicago, Illinois: Moody Press, 1967.

Kidner, Derek. *Genesis.* Downers Grove, Illinois: InterVarsity Press, 1967.

Mackintosh, C. H. *Genesis to Deuteronomy.* Neptune, New Jersey: Loizeaux Brothers, 1972.

Meyer, F. B. *Abraham: The Obedience of Faith.* Fort Washington, Pennsylvania: Christian Literature Crusade, n.d.

Meyer, F. B. *Israel: A Prince With God.* Fort Washington, Pennsylvania: Christian Literature Crusade, n.d.

Meyer, F. B. *Joseph: Beloved—Hated—Exalted.* Fort Washington, Pennsylvania: Christian Literature Crusade, n.d.

Morgan, G. Campbell. *The Unfolding Message of the Bible*. Old Tappan, New Jersey: Fleming H. Revell Company, n.d.

Morris, Henry M. *The Genesis Record: A Scientific and Devotional Commentary*. Grand Rapids, Michigan: Baker Book House, 1976.

Morris, Henry M. and Whitcomb, John C., Jr. *The Genesis Flood*. Grand Rapids, Michigan: Baker Book House, 1961.

Pink, Arthur W. *Gleanings in Genesis*. Chicago, Illinois: Moody Press, 1922.

Stigers, Harold. *A Commentary on Genesis*. Grand Rapids, Michigan: Zondervan Publishing House, 1975.

Thomas, W. H. Griffith. *Genesis: A Devotional Commentary*. Grand Rapids, Michigan: Eerdmans Publishing Company, 1946.

Unger, Merrill F. *Unger's Commentary on the Old Testament*. Vol. 1. Chicago, Illinois: Moody Press, 1981.

Vos, Howard F. *Genesis*. Chicago, Illinois: Moody Press, 1980.

Wood, Leon J. *Genesis: A Study Guide Commentary*. Grand Rapids, Michigan: Zondervan Publishing House, 1975.

For additional material on creation, the Flood, and science, write to:

Institute for Creation Research
10946 Woodside Ave. North
Santee, California 92071